THE GOOD COOK

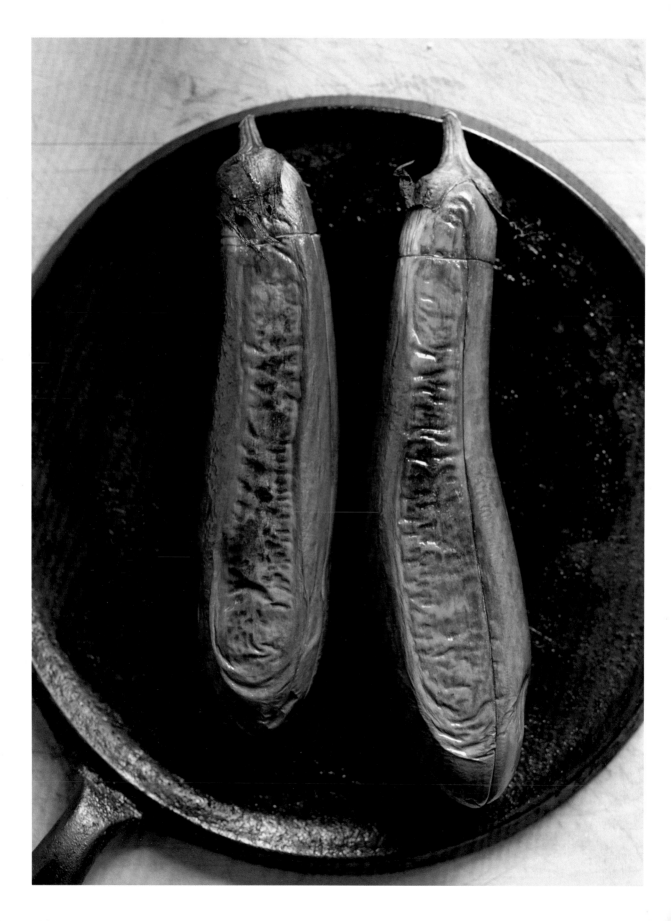

THE
GOOD
COOK

SIMON
HOPKINSON

BBC
BOOKS

This book is published to accompany the television series entitled *The Good Cook*, first broadcast on BBC1 in 2011.

Executive Producers: Pete Lawrence and Simon Knight
Series Producer: Simon Kerfoot

10 9 8 7 6 5 4 3 2 1

The Random House Group Limited Reg. No. 954009

Addresses for companies within the Random House Group can be found at www.randomhouse.co.uk

A CIP catalogue record for this book is available from the British Library.

ISBN 978 1 849 90228 1

The Random House Group Limited supports the Forest Stewardship Council (FSC), the leading international forest certification organisation. All our titles that are printed on Greenpeace-approved FSC-certified paper carry the FSC logo. Our paper procurement policy can be found at www.rbooks.co.uk/environment

Commissioning editor: Muna Reyal
Project editor: Laura Higginson
Copy-editor: Annie Lee
Designer: Will Webb
Photography: Jason Lowe
Production: Helen Everson

Colour origination by AltaImage, London
Printed and bound in Germany by Firmengruppe APPL, aprinta druck, Wemding

To buy books by your favourite authors and register for offers, visit www.rbooks.co.uk

for Anthony Goff

Contents

Introduction

For me, cookery is a pleasure that is also a part of daily life. It is an ongoing process; a regular pursuit, if you like, whether it is associated with work, as it is for me, or as a continuing process for a couple or family where food just happens as habit and necessity. In time, a build-up of all kinds of cooking components will evolve as you proceed, but frankly, to make it a real pleasure, what is essential, above some care and consideration, is a 'wish' rather than a 'need' to cook.

Some cooks regularly pronounce that you can't really go wrong as long as you have fabulous ingredients. Well, I'm not so sure … I will shop anywhere, always have. I may well splash out on fab stuff from time to time, also making occasional trips to a farmer's market, but I become equally excited by a vacuum-packed bargain breast of lamb from the supermarket because I know I can make it taste very good (see Lovely Lamb). I guess it is simply a need to do things well; get things right. The cooking itself is all, for me.

Stocks can – and will – appear on a regular basis from poultry carcase and meat bone, with various seasonal soups naturally following on from this happy chore. Leftover meat stews may be turned into pasta sauces, ravioli fillings (for when you get serious) and, of course, something such as a lovely cottage pie. Maybe roast a larger Sunday chicken than you need, then cook a creamed pie filling with what's left, plus mushrooms and bits of ham, say. It doesn't necessarily need to be for Monday; wrapped-up, cold roast chicken will keep in the fridge for four to five days, so make it when you are happy to, for if you really love to cook then time will always be found. Is the true opera lover ever too busy not to go to the opera?

It may not necessarily be a composed meal in the traditional sense that I prepare these days, and I don't always consider that a dish needs anything to accompany it as a matter of course. Take, for example, the photograph of the dainty dish of kipper baked with tomato and cream that is attached to this introduction. I had frozen a kipper (can't remember why) and, as a result of that, realised it was probably not going to taste quite as good if simply cooked in its own right for breakfast. As I peered into the fridge, there was half a pot of cream and also the remnants of a carton of cherry toms.

So, boiling water was briefly poured over the kipper, its flesh eased from whiskery bones and popped into a couple of buttered, shallow dishes. A large pinch of curry powder went into the cream plus a healthy spoonful of mustard powder, then all was whisked together. Finally, this mixture was poured over the fish and halved toms, baked in the oven until the cream blistered, and eaten with a spoon. The first attempt was a little too liquid, but I have now refined it (the final recipe is on page 113). However, I cannot think of a nicer supper or luxurious weekend breakfast than this delightfully complete little number. More often than not, it can be just a few bits and pieces that surprise and please most when the thinking is sound.

Favourite stalwart ingredients such as the familiar large jar of oily, salted anchovies will always nudge me in summer. Here, I will embrace the sunny south of France in a mélange of ripe and red tomatoes, the fruitiest olive oil and all the other fragrant components that complete a perfect salade niçoise. A lump of Parmesan (always, but always in my fridge) is forever in attendance for the moment when possibly the most perfectly plain of risotti is exactly what one needs to eat; just cheese, butter, rice, stock ... and much excited stirring. But when I am feeling cosy and slow, another, more familial cheese will beckon, nothing more than that of a deeply savoury Lancashire cheese and onion pie of the sort my mother used to make; all warm and wet with melted curds and slippery allium, there is little else imaginable which I would rather cook at that moment.

When all is said and done, I just cook. It really is what I do. Day in, day out, I cook for me at home. Occasionally, I will share the results with one or two close chums, but only ever for lunch. One of the things I also really enjoy, however, is cooking for – and with – friends in their home, in *their* kitchen, when staying over for a weekend, say. It is lucky for me, in general, that these like-minded chums have the most serviceable of kitchens, but I can cook anywhere if quietly pushed. Possibly the finest ratatouille I ever assembled was prepared over a Calor gas camping flame in the mountains above Nice, in the south of France.

You may or may not know, but the cookery book that you have in your hands was inspired by a performance, by a cook on television: me. I am astonished to have written that sentence at all, as the very idea of TV was always anathema to me. Even worse was the prospect of looking into what I had always referred to as 'that terrible black hole' (the camera lens) while also cooking and speaking at one and the same time.

'Are you quite mad?' I would exclaim to folk who had suggested on various occasions that I might, possibly, be better than I thought at doing a turn on TV. 'No, really,' they would ridiculously insist, 'we think you could be quite good. You have something to say.' Well, eventually, this timid cook did decide to say something. And it was difficult learning to say anything, let alone cook at the same time. I mean, it isn't exactly a natural pastime for one who usually just gets on with his daily dalliance – albeit a serious one – pleasing himself with some well-chosen culinary pleasures while listening to Radio 4. I can only hope that both the visual result and this book may, possibly, quietly urge on a similar need to perform just a few new dalliances of your own, in kitchen.

And, you know what? I had a ball staring into that terrible black hole.

anchovy & aubergine

anchovy & onion tarts

....

serves 4–6, as nibbles

40g butter

2 large onions, halved, then thinly sliced

200ml port or Marsala

1 tsp redcurrant jelly

3 tbsp red wine vinegar

salt

200g (approx.) all-butter puff pastry

20–25 anchovy fillets,
  cut in half lengthways

herbes de Provence

cayenne pepper

....

These incredibly delicious little munchies are inspired by a little taster the chef Pierre Koffmann used to serve at his original, very small and railway-carriage-thin Tante Claire restaurant in Chelsea, London. I recall eating these as long ago as 1980 and thinking, then, that they were one of the most delicious things I had ever put in my mouth. The following recipe is my interpretation of that original, thirty-year-old memory.

If you are an avid pasta maker, you may well own a pasta-rolling machine. If so, then this apparatus is ideal for rolling the pastry as thin as possible. If not, however, just do the very best you can with a rolling pin. If using the pasta machine, take the pastry up to notch number 5.

Melt the butter in a heavy-based pot and add the onions. Slowly cook them, stirring regularly, until well softened and just beginning to colour – about 25–30 minutes. Add the port/Marsala, jelly, vinegar and very little salt. Bring up to a simmer, then reduce until all the liquid has completely evaporated; a heat diffuser pad placed underneath towards the end of the reduction will help prevent any scorching. Scrape into a bowl and cool completely.

Preheat the oven to 200°C/400°F/gas mark 6.

Cut the pastry into 4 equal pieces. Roll each one out into a rectangle about 25cm long by 10cm wide – and as thinly as possible. Lightly grease a large, flat baking tray, lay the pastry sheets on it and prick them all over with a fork. Put the whole

tray into the freezer until the pastry is stiff and firm. (If you have a second flat baking tray, place this in the oven now to heat up; this will help the underneath of the pastry to become good and crisp while baking.)

Remove the baking tray from the freezer and, using a palette knife, quickly spread each sheet of pastry with a thin layer of the onion mixture, leaving a 0.5cm gap around the edge. Following the length of the pastry rectangle, lay a half anchovy fillet at approximately 1.5cm intervals. Lightly sprinkle with the herbs and cayenne pepper. Bake in the oven (on the preheated baking tray) for 8–10 minutes, then loosely cover with a piece of kitchen foil and continue baking for a further 5 minutes or so; this is to prevent the anchovies scorching. Carefully lift the pastries from the tray and lay on a cooling rack until warm.

To serve, place the pastries on a chopping surface and, with a sharp, heavy-bladed knife, deftly slice equally between the anchovies to form little pastry fingers. Serve without delay, and with drinks. Excellent with ice-cold Martinis.

spinach & ricotta croquettes with anchovy sauce

....

serves 4
for the croquettes
750g spinach
120g ricotta
3 egg yolks, beaten
75g grated Parmesan
freshly grated nutmeg, to taste
salt and freshly ground black pepper
oil, for frying
plain flour
1 egg, beaten
100–125g fine breadcrumbs

for the anchovy sauce
  (makes approx. 250ml)
200g unsalted butter
3 egg yolks
1 tbsp water
1 x 50g tin of anchovy fillets, drained of oil
lemon juice to taste
a few shakes of Tabasco sauce

....

These soft and creamy morsels are loosely based upon an Italian gnocchi recipe, but with an added coating to give an interesting, contrasting crunch. I know that it is a curiously off-putting comparison, but the result of this bread-crumbed coating is as important to this dish as is the crisp coating one finds on a proper chocolate truffle that has been hand-dipped into melted chocolate, so that it has that deliciously crisp bite to it beneath the final cocoa dusting. Chocolate truffles that have only been rolled in cocoa are not, as far as I am concerned, chocolate truffles at all. Incidentally, do try not to think of chocolate when you are tasting spinach and anchovy...

Blanch the spinach briefly in boiling water. Drain, then refresh in ice-cold water. Squeeze in a tea towel until dry. Using a food processor, purée together the spinach, ricotta, egg yolks, Parmesan, nutmeg, a little salt and plenty of pepper until well amalgamated, but not too smooth. Spread on a shallow tray, press clingfilm over the surface and allow to firm up in the fridge for a minimum of 2 hours.
To make the sauce, melt the butter and pour it into a heated jug (fill with boiled

water, then discard), then keep moderately hot. Place the yolks in a small food processor or similar, add the water and whiz until pale and creamy. With the motor running, pour in the melted butter in a thin stream, but leaving most of the milky residue behind in the jug, until glossy and thick. Add the drained anchovies, a touch of lemon juice and further process until smooth and tasty. Now spike with Tabasco to taste. Keep the sauce warm while the croquettes are cooking. (Note: if you feel that the sauce is really too thick, then a little of that milky residue may be added as a final loosener.)

Heat the oil for frying in either a solid, deep pan or, for the absolute ease of it, an electric deep-fryer. Either way, aim for about 160–170°C, or when a small piece of bread turns pale golden in about a minute. Form the spinach mixture into oval shapes with the help of two dessertspoons. Briefly roll in the flour, then in the beaten egg and finally coat in breadcrumbs. Work quickly, as the mixture can quickly soften. You should finish with 3 or 4 croquettes per person, depending upon spoon size.

Deep-fry the croquettes for 4–5 minutes (in batches, so as not to overcrowd the deep-fryer or pan), drain on kitchen paper and keep warm in a low oven. Serve forthwith, accompanied by the anchovy sauce.

salade niçoise

....

serves any number...

....

When I first wrote a recipe for this much-debated salad (about seventeen years ago), I was not a great fan of tinned tuna; I could only see it as a kind of upmarket catfood. But, truly, good processed tuna was hard to find anywhere in those days, unless you had access to big-city Italian or Spanish delis, say. So, it was not until I discovered the delights of the Spanish brand Ortíz, and their *bonito ventresca* (tuna belly) packed in olive oil, that I was finally enlightened to how delicious such tinned fish can be. Their anchovy fillets, too, are among the very best I have tasted.

That which I insisted upon for my salad, then, was for the tuna to be ditched in favour of an increase in anchovies; which, in fact, I could still stand by, so much do I love them. However, this belly stuff is quite marvellous, separating into soft, fatty pieces when nudged by the thumb, falling over the surface of the salad in pale pink flakes.

For once, I have decided not to give this recipe in a conventional manner. It is entirely up to you how much, or how little of each ingredient you wish to use. However, apart from *the fishes*, you should not omit the following four items: *tomatoes, boiled eggs, black olives* and *olive oil* – preferably French, niçoise even better (the most admired local brand, Alziari, in its colourful tin, is very good, if pricey). Also, try to obtain tiny little niçoise olives. The tomatoes, naturally, should be ripe, deeply flavoured and heavy with juice. If you have chosen plum tomatoes, core and quarter them, and, if they are large, cut them possibly into sixths, or even eighths.

Choose good, large eggs that you know will have a deep orange yolk – simply because they will look fab in the salad – but that are not absolutely fresh (difficult to peel). Place them in a pan of cold water, bring up to a definite boil and then switch off the heat. Cover, leave for 5 minutes, then cool under a cold running tap for 2–3 minutes. This method will give a white that isn't rubbery, together with a yolk that is soft in the centre. Best quartered.

Other garnishes to add to the tuna and/or anchovies, together with the essential tomatoes, eggs, olives and their oil, can vary widely – and by whim, to a certain extent. Personally, I favour peeled and sliced *cucumber*; thinly sliced bulbous *spring onions*; large, old-fashioned blowsy *capers* rather than tiny tots, but never those dreadful caper berries; very thin *haricots verts*, topped and tailed, quickly boiled until tender, not crunchy. Small, super-fresh, tender *broad beans* and *artichokes*, both raw, trimmed and sliced, may further be included during their brief season. I used to add sliced new potatoes too, but went off the idea some years ago, now.

If you insist upon a few salad leaves (I remain ambivalent here) simply because it is called a 'salad', just use the very inner leaves of a *soft round lettuce*, nothing more, as a rumpled bed upon which to rest the other salad components. And if you want herbs somewhere, add *basil* and maybe some *feathery chervil* to sprinkle over the finished dish as little sprigs. It adds a pleasing, faintly aniseed note, so particular to the Côte d'Azur. Finally, I need the *merest whiff of garlic* somewhere, though some might vehemently disagree, and do. A clove or two crushed and infused in the olive oil, then discarded, is a delicate notion.

To serve the salade niçoise, nicely arrange the ingredients in a shallow, white dish in a way that pleases you most. Liberally dress with olive oil (garlic-infused, or not) and the merest trickle of *red wine vinegar*, then season with care. And, by the way, to use a slice of rare-grilled fresh tuna in this salad is a notion only to be entertained by the permanently bewildered.

aubergines with olive oil, garlic, parsley & feta cheese

serves 4

4 long, thin-skinned purple aubergines,
   or 2 large, more common
   black-skinned ones

1–2 cloves of garlic, finely chopped

a handful of parsley leaves, finely chopped

5–6 tbsp very fine, extra virgin olive oil

a little sea salt and freshly ground
   black pepper

100–150g feta cheese (best if barrel-aged)

lemons, to taste

My friend Lindsey Bareham kindly gave me this recipe. Every year, when she and a friend holiday on the Greek island of Lemnos, they enjoy their daily lunch and swim at a seaside village called Thanos, at Harry's beachside taverna. After many requests, she eventually wheedled the recipe out of Harry, who is, all at once, cook, gardener and proprietor. I am most grateful to LB, for this is one of the very best – if not *the* best – aubergine dishes I have ever cooked and eaten. The magical moments of the dish are both its quiet simplicity, and the elemental fact, for once, of allowing the aubergine to taste exactly of itself. It further goes without saying that the oil should be very good indeed.

The very best aubergines for this dish are the long, pale purple ones, most often found in Asian stores. Their skins are nice and thin, resulting in a more thrifty discard, once peeled. The flavour is also very good, and don't be put off by any seeds; they certainly don't detract from the finished dish by any means. Also, it is well worth noting that when adding garlic and parsley to this kind of dish, the end result is doubly aromatic if you finely chop the two together. In French cookery, this is known as 'persillade'.

Heat an overhead grill to medium hot. Run a small, sharp knife round the neck of each aubergine, a centimetre or so below the stalk and only just cutting through the skin. Then make 4 evenly spaced, shallow cuts along the length of the aubergine right down to the bulbous end. Grill them, turning every 5–7 minutes or so, until evenly cooked and the aubergine feels soft but not too collapsed within. In the case of the purple aubergines, their skins will also have turned a dull brown colour.

Transfer to a large, oval white plate and allow to cool for a couple of minutes. Now, using a small knife, deftly lift off the skin in 4 long, narrow sheets and discard (this peeling affair is an extremely pleasurable task). Without cutting right through the stalk end, cut the aubergine in half lengthways and gently prise apart until you have 2 horizontal halves, but remaining attached at the top end; a kind of elongated heart shape, if you like. Mix the garlic and parsley with the olive oil and spoon over the assembly. Season lightly with salt (the cheese is salty anyway) and pepper, crumble feta cheese over the top and squeeze over some lemon juice. If necessary, trickle over more olive oil to finish. Serve warm, or at room temperature.

aubergines parmigiana

serves 4

for the sauce (makes about 1 litre)

2kg ripe plum tomatoes

1 whole head of garlic, each clove
    peeled and then bruised

2 bay leaves

leaves from 1 head of fresh green
    celery or 2 sticks of celery, chopped

thinly pared zest of 1 small lemon

2 tsp sugar

a little salt

2 large aubergines, peeled and sliced
    into 2cm thick discs

approx. 125–150ml olive oil

salt and freshly ground black pepper

2–3 large ladles of homemade tomato sauce
    (see below)

12–15 basil leaves

2 buffalo mozzarella, thinly sliced

3–4 tbsp freshly grated Parmesan

One of the best loved of all Italian aubergine dishes, but particularly so, it seems, in the US, especially in traditional, old-fashioned Italian restaurants in New York City, where the word is 'eggplant' – as, in fact, it is in all other English-speaking nations in the world except here. I guess it is the proximity to France, but I have always been perplexed by this. And, by the way, the full pronunciation of this dish by most North Americans is, phonetically, 'eggplant parmajahn'.

Before making this recipe, you will need to make some tomato sauce. It is quite clear that there is too much for your needs in this recipe, but it is much better to make it in large quantities and, furthermore, it freezes well. Use small, lidded plastic pots.

Plunge the tomatoes into boiling water, leave for a few seconds, then drain, cool in iced water and peel off the skins. Put all the sauce ingredients into a heavy-bottomed pan and bring to a simmer. Allow to cook very gently for 1–1½ hours, stirring from time to time. As the final sauce consistency should be a bit sloppy and still just pourable, take from the heat before it looks too thick. Personally, I like to first use a vegetable mill (mouli-légumes), using the finest disc, and then force the resultant sauce through a sieve, pressing down well with the back of a small ladle.

Preheat the oven to 200°C/400°F/gas mark 6.

Put the aubergines into a large roasting tin and evenly douse with olive oil, while turning them over in your hands (the best way); you may not need all the oil, but they should be well coated. Season with salt.

Gently cook the aubergines in a large, dry, non-stick frying pan over a moderate heat in batches, turning once, until each side is a rich, golden brown and soft to the touch. Transfer to another tray lined with kitchen paper, to both cool and let any excess oil be absorbed by the paper.

Now, take a large, deep dish – which will be nice enough to go from stove to table – and cover the base with a ladleful of tomato sauce. Cover this with a single layer of aubergines, then a few basil leaves, torn, and followed by slices of mozzarella to roughly match the aubergine slices beneath. Also, grind over some pepper as you go. Repeat this layer, finishing with a thin layer of tomato sauce and more torn basil leaves. Generously sprinkle the surface with Parmesan. Bake in the oven for 30 minutes or so, or until bubbling at the edges and a gorgeous-looking golden brown on top, with nicely blistered pustules here and there. Leave to cool for about 10–15 minutes before serving, as dishes such as these can often be incendiary within.

aubergines & tomatoes with homemade masala paste

serves 4

for the masala paste

4 tbsp cumin seeds

2 tbsp coriander seeds

2 tsp whole cloves

1 dsp fennel seeds

1 dsp brown mustard seeds

1 dsp small dried red chillies

a small handful of curry leaves
  (fresh or dried)

300g onions, peeled and chopped

125g garlic cloves, peeled and chopped

150g ginger, peeled and chopped

2 tbsp tamarind paste

2 tsp turmeric

2 tbsp red wine vinegar

100g creamed coconut

2 tsp Maldon salt

1 dsp caster sugar

4 long, thin-skinned purple aubergines,
  or 2 large, more common
  black-skinned ones

approx. 100ml vegetable oil

salt

8 small tomatoes, or 4 large
  (ripe beef tomatoes, say),
  cored and thinly sliced

2 cloves of garlic, bruised

1–1½ tbsp masala paste, or to taste
  (see below)

lemon or lime juice, to taste

chopped coriander (optional)

I am so sorry, but once again a very important component of the following recipe has to be made before the dish can be completed: a homemade Indian masala paste. However, I promise that you will be glad to have it around – and it keeps for weeks and weeks in the fridge.

Using a non-stick frying pan, lightly toast the whole spices – cumin, coriander, cloves, fennel, mustard and chillies – until smelling quite wonderful and pungent, but be careful not to burn them. Tip into a small bowl to cool. In a food processor place the curry leaves, onions, garlic, ginger, tamarind paste, turmeric, vinegar, coconut, salt and sugar. Once the spices are cool, process these in a coffee grinder, or similar, until powdered. Add to the other ingredients in the food processor and work everything until as smooth as possible; this will depend on the sharpness of your blade and the power of the machine. Do not be tempted to add the spices whole, as they will remain 'bitty' if not previously powdered.

There is enough here to fill 2 small glass jars of approx. 350ml capacity. Cover with a film of oil, put on a lid and store in the fridge until needed. Each time you use some, smooth over the surface once more, then cover with a little more oil to seal.

So, now to make the dish itself...

Preheat an overhead grill.

Cut the aubergines in half lengthways and criss-cross the open surfaces with a small, sharp knife, about halfway down into the flesh. Generously brush with oil and season with salt. Place under the grill, not too close, and allow to cook through until golden, soft within and very slightly sunken. Cool slightly, then cover the surfaces with overlapping sliced tomatoes. Keep the grill active, but at a lower temperature.

Warm about 4–5 tablespoons of oil with the garlic and 1½ tablespoons of the masala paste for a few minutes. Fish out the garlic and then spoon the flavoured oil over the tomato-topped aubergine halves. Return to the grill – again, not too close – and cook until the tomatoes are well burnished and the spices are smelling deliciously aromatic. Serve with lemon or lime juice squeezed over together with some chopped coriander, if you like. Very good indeed eaten with a bowl of super-cool yoghurt mixed with some freshly chopped mint.

cool cucumber, hot horseradish, bitter endive

cucumber

fried cucumber with soured cream & dill

serves 2

for the dill salting mixture
3 tbsp sea salt
1 tbsp dill seed
2 tsp sugar

for the cucumber
200–225g cucumber, cut into
   thick (0.5cm) slices, unpeeled
1 tsp dill salting mixture (see below)
oil, for frying
1 tbsp self-raising flour
1 tbsp potato flour (or cornflour)
¼ tsp baking powder
approx. 100ml iced water
a little plain flour, for dusting

for the soured cream and dill
150ml soured cream
a pinch or 2 of the dill salting mixture
   (see below), or to taste
1 dsp freshly chopped dill
pinch of cayenne pepper

I am indebted to my friend and fellow cook Stephen Markwick for kindly introducing me to this lovely, unusual and dainty dish (who would ever have thought of deep-frying cucumber at all?). I first enjoyed it in his restaurant and deli, Culinaria, in Bristol, which he runs with his wife, Judy.

Stephen is one of the very best cooks I know, having that rare, intellectual understanding of how food can taste exactly right, and the description 'honest cook' could not be more apt where Mr Markwick is concerned. I can only hope that he won't mind that I have fiddled about a bit with his original instructions; it is what interested cooks do, after all...

First make the dill salting mixture. Simply grind the 3 ingredients together in a small food processor or grinder, until well blended; the dill seeds are tough little

blighters and I have found that they just won't pulverise completely, but no matter. Stored in a well-sealed jar in a cool, dark cupboard, the mixture will keep for weeks – but not for ever, naturally, as the dill flavour will dissipate over time. Let us say about 3 months.

Place the cucumber slices in a shallow dish and sprinkle over 1 teaspoon of the dill salting mixture. Mix together well by hand, then leave to salt for at least 1 hour, turning the slices over and over from time to time. Do not drain. Meanwhile, make the soured cream and dill. Just mix the ingredients together in a small bowl and keep in the fridge until needed.

You will need to heat the oil for frying the cucumber in either a solid, deep pan or, for the absolute ease of it, an electric deep-fryer. Either way, aim for around about 180°C, or when a small piece of bread turns pale golden in about a minute. Mix together both the flours and the baking powder in a bowl and whisk in the iced water until you have a smooth batter. Leave to sit for 20 minutes.

To fry the cucumber, lift out the slices directly from the dish, and do NOT rinse or dry them. Dust the slices first in the plain flour, then dip them into the batter. Fry for about 3–4 minutes, turning occasionally, until pale golden and crisp. Drain on kitchen paper for a few moments before serving with the cool sauce.

You may wish to do the frying in 2 batches, but I would suggest rather that you eat the first batch, then cook a second batch. Eating two crisp and hot servings is far better than one serving crisp, and one not so crisp, eaten at the same time.

tzatziki

makes about 750g – or a generous bowlful

2 medium cucumbers, peeled

2 tsp salt

500g tub of full-fat Greek yoghurt

1 tbsp white wine vinegar or, if you
  prefer, the juice of 1 lemon

2 large cloves of garlic, crushed
  and finely chopped

5–6 tbsp extra virgin olive oil

freshly ground black pepper, plenty

2 heaped tbsp finely chopped dill,
  or mint, if you prefer

More dill! – in this evergreen Greek favourite. The son of my friends Robert and Jane Sackville-West, the honourable Arthur, aged eleven, almost cannot sit down to lunch without there being a large bowl of tzatziki nearby, and most excellently made by his mother. The boy, however, won't countenance the merest whisker of dill in it, but then dill is a difficult taste for many grown-ups, too; those so afflicted should take the mint route.

Tzatziki is one of my most favourite ways with cucumber; so cooling and fragrant that it quite fills a dining room with its scent – especially if you grow your own, as does Lady Sackville. His Lordship barbecues a mean butterflied leg of lamb, too, and tzatziki goes particularly well with this. Have some with the marinated butterflied leg of lamb on page 129.

Coarsely grate the cucumbers and sprinkle over the salt. Mix well, put into a colander and suspend over a deep bowl. Leave to soak and drip for at least 1 hour – or a bit longer, it doesn't matter. Manually, squeeze out as much moisture as you can from the cucumber, then place it in a bowl and mix in the yoghurt, vinegar (or lemon juice), garlic, almost all the oil, the pepper and the dill (or mint). Decant into a serving dish and chill in the fridge for at least 30 minutes. When serving, trickle over a little more olive oil and grind over some extra pepper. Always serve very cold.

horseradish

horseradish base recipe

200g horseradish root, peeled
and finely grated
2–3 tbsp water
5 tbsp lemon juice

2 tsp Maldon salt
1½ tbsp caster sugar
salt

I have been a fan of fresh horseradish since I was a boy. Even though it shocked my sinuses and made Dad cry while he was grating it, I couldn't get enough of it – almost in a masochistic way. But I just adored the taste! Even now, I would rather not eat Sunday roast beef if there isn't any creamed horseradish to hand. And lots of it, too.

The following can be made up, stored in a Kilner jar, say, and kept in the fridge for a few weeks. Just occasionally, it loses its nice cream colour and takes on a kind of pale grey hue, but this never seems to affect the flavour. By the way, never attempt to process large lumps of horseradish root in a food processor without grating it first, as it turns horribly bitter. Don't ask me why this is so, but hand grating seems the only way. If you find the tears really streaming down, try grating the root near an open window, so that the draught wafts the odours past your eyes.

So, here is the base recipe for all horseradish condiments:

Put everything into a small food processor and grind until smoothish. Decant into a sealable jar and store in the fridge until needed.

smoked salmon & chive potato pancakes with horseradish cream

serves 4 as a first course

for the horseradish cream

2 tbsp horseradish base recipe
(see page 41)
100ml double cream

for the smoked salmon filling

125g smoked salmon
(offcuts are fine, here)
1 tbsp finely chopped chives
2 tbsp soured cream
a little freshly ground pepper

for the potato pancake batter

300g potatoes, peeled and cut
into large chunks
40ml milk
40g plain flour, sieved
2 eggs
2 egg whites
1½ tbsp double cream
salt and freshly ground black pepper
2–3 tbsp clarified butter, for frying
(see below)

I love these dear little beauties. Granted, they can be a little bit tricky to make first time round, but once you have the knack they are fun to do. And very delicious to boot – or there wouldn't be much point, would there?

You will need to make some clarified butter for cooking the pancakes. This is simple (and useful to have around anyway) and fashioned thus:

Melt a packet of unsalted butter. Skim off the froth with a spoon. Carefully pour out the clear butter – which lies beneath the froth and the milky residue below – into a bowl, while leaving the milky stuff behind. Discard both froth and residue. Voilà, clarified butter. The leftover butter should be poured into a small pot, covered and kept in the fridge for another day. It will keep for 2–3 weeks. Or freeze it, of course.

To make the horseradish cream, simply whisk both the ingredients together until thickened.

For the filling, finely chop the smoked salmon and, in a small bowl, mix together with the chives, soured cream and pepper. Put into the fridge to keep cool, but remove about 10 minutes before you begin to make the pancakes.

For the pancakes, preferably steam the potatoes (or boil carefully, drain and allow to dry out over a low heat for a few minutes). While they are still hot, put them through a mouli-légumes (or a potato ricer) on the finest setting. Transfer to a mixing bowl and allow to cool. Now beat in the milk, flour, eggs, egg whites, cream and seasoning.

Preheat an overhead grill. Gently heat a little of the clarified butter in a large-ish, preferably non-stick frying pan. Pour in 4 tablespoons of batter, with a decent space between them. Once there is a pale browning at the edges of the pancakes and a few tiny bubbles on the surface – this will take about 30 seconds – spoon a little of the smoked salmon mixture into the middle of each pancake and only just push it into the surface. Now, carefully add a little more batter, but only enough to cover the salmon completely. Immediately, place the pan under the grill for 20–30 seconds or so, to set the surface; the texture should be slightly springy to the touch, but still moist within.

Remove from the grill and quickly flip the pancakes over with a palette knife on to a warm plate. Keep them warm while you make another 4 pancakes. If you like, brush them with a little clarified butter before topping each one with a teaspoon of the horseradish cream.

horseradish & beetroot relish for salt ox tongue

serves 4, with enough for seconds

1 small salted ox tongue, approx. 1kg,
   well washed in cold running water
   for 5 minutes

2 carrots, peeled and cut in half lengthways

3 onions, one stuck with 4 cloves

4 sticks of celery, cut into short lengths

2 bay leaves

3 sprigs of thyme

a few peppercorns

for the horseradish and beetroot

3 medium-sized cooked beetroots,
   peeled and cut into chunks

3–4 tbsp horseradish base recipe
   (see page 41)

1 tbsp balsamic vinegar

1 level tbsp caster sugar

salt, to taste

This relish is just fabulous with all boiled (perhaps poached is a more apt and delicate description) meats – and especially salted ones; and particularly good alongside boiled salt brisket, or even gammon or a bacon joint. I have, most successfully, poached tongue and brisket together before now, which makes for a hearty duet, it should be said. For some reason, the reaction between the beetroot and horseradish, once processed, is a powerful one, so please look out for your nose when you open the lid of the machine.

Put the tongue into a roomy pot and cover with water to a depth of about 5cm. Bring to the boil and remove any resultant scum as it forms on the surface. Now add the vegetables, herbs and peppercorns and simmer for about 2–2½ hours, or until the tongue is cooked; insert a skewer through the thickest part of the meat, and if there is no resistance, the tongue is done. Keep hot in the cooking liquor until ready to serve. (The vegetables may be discarded, as they have become exhausted and given up all their flavour to the broth.)

Meanwhile, make the horseradish and beetroot relish by working all the ingredients together in a food processor until smooth-ish.

To serve, take the tongue from its liquor and remove the skin with a small knife. Slice the tongue and lay on a heated platter with, or without, some of its cooking liquor. Serve the beetroot and horseradish alongside. Creamed potatoes, or buttery boiled potatoes turned through some finely chopped parsley, are the order of the day here.

endive

endives au gratin

....

serves 4 as a first course, or 2 for supper

50g butter

4 large endives, trimmed of any tired,
  outer leaves and the base core
  removed in a cone shape, using
  a small, sharp knife

salt and freshly ground black pepper

juice of 1 lemon

4 thin slices of cooked ham
  (smoked, if you like)

for the cheese sauce

30g butter

20g flour

225ml cold milk from the fridge

30g grated Gruyère

40g grated Parmesan

salt, white pepper and a scraping
  of nutmeg

....

I am extremely fond of cooked endives. Or chicory, if you like, but as I was
brought up as an apprentice in a French kitchen, it will always be endive
with me, as it was the first place I saw them. The first thing that astonished
me was the way they quietly cooked away without any added liquid apart from
a splash of lemon juice. And what makes it even more curious is how lemon
juice actually imparts a sweetness to the vegetable when it's braised with
butter. Naturally, however, when you consider that this firm little torpedo is,
essentially, a tight bundle of salad leaves, the water content is bound to be high;
the thing just oozes out its deliciously astringent juices into the pan as it
putters away. Bitter, here, is good.

Preheat the oven to 170°C/325°F/gas mark 3.

Use a solid-bottomed pot with a lid, making sure that it will take the endives
in a single layer.

Melt the butter and cook until foaming. Put in the endives, turning them
thoroughly in the butter, then season. Turn the heat down to low and gently colour
the endives on all sides until well glossed and golden. Add the lemon juice and turn
up the heat a little. Cover, and place in the oven for 30 minutes.

Meanwhile, make the sauce. Melt the butter in a saucepan, stir in the flour, cook gently for a few minutes but keep the roux pale coloured. Pour in the cold milk (this is important) all in one go, whisking together thoroughly, then place the pan over a very low heat, stirring constantly until beginning to thicken; although there should not be any, the odd lump that forms will, eventually, disappear into the sauce. Add all the Gruyère, 25g of the Parmesan, the seasonings, and allow to simmer very gently indeed (a diffuser pad is useful), stirring occasionally, for about 10–15 minutes; slow cooking makes for a good cheese sauce – and all béchamel-based sauces, in fact. Cover, and keep warm.

Now, take the endives from the oven, remove the lid and turn them over. Cover once more and cook for a further 20–30 minutes or so; it is relatively difficult to overcook this delicious vegetable, and I quite like a braised endive to be a bit sticky and have crusted edges. If you too like this idea, then remove the lid for the last 10 minutes of cooking time. Furthermore, there is nothing worse than an endive that is firm in the middle. (Many recipes I read inform the cook that an endive can braise in 20 minutes. This is poppycock.) Increase the heat of the oven to 200°C/400°F/gas mark 6.

To finish the dish, roll each endive in a slice of ham and lay in a lightly greased, shallow baking dish. Cover with the sauce and sprinkle over the remaining Parmesan. Cook on the top shelf of the oven for about 15–20 minutes, or until the sauce is bubbling around the edges and the surface is nicely blistered; flash under a hot grill for a few seconds, if you like.

pot-roast pork with endives

serves 3–4

700g boned pork loin, rind removed

salt and freshly ground black pepper

a smear of lard, dripping or olive oil

a thick slice of butter

4 large endives, trimmed of
   any tired, outer leaves and the base
   core removed in a cone shape, using
   a small, sharp knife

2 shallots, chopped

300ml dry cider

the merest splash of cider vinegar

3 sprigs of sage

2 cloves of garlic, bruised

There are two pale meats that have always been happy eating partners with the endive: veal is very good indeed, as is the following pork. However, when the chosen joint is cooked together with the endive as an ensemble, the marriage is one of the very best and most loved – at least it is, by this cook. The cider sweetens the dish in the most agreeable manner.

Preheat the oven to 170°C/325°F/gas mark 3.

Season the pork loin and colour in the lard, dripping or olive oil in a solid-bottomed pot over a moderate heat, until golden all over. Lift out the meat and put it on a plate. Add the butter to the pot and, when beginning to froth, introduce the endives and similarly colour until they, too, are golden. Tip in the shallots and mingle them around a bit. Now push the endives to the sides of the pot and replace the pork in the middle. Pour in the cider and add the vinegar, tuck in the sage sprigs and pop in the garlic cloves. Slide into the oven and cook, initially, for about 30 minutes. Remove the pot, turn over the pork, and cook for a further 30 minutes.

During this time, the cider will reduce somewhat, the endives will soften and, of course, the pork will cook. The hour should do it, but the liquid will probably still be a touch too thin. So, turn off the oven, remove the meat and endives (they should be very soft), keep warm in the oven's waning heat with the door ajar, and place the

pot over a lively heat. Reduce the liquid until a touch more syrupy, but don't overdo it; over-salty and over-sweet you don't want.

To serve, slice the pork on to a heated platter, garnish with the endives and spoon the sauce over – it must be said – this rather monotone assembly. However, be assured, it is a tasty dish with great charm.

cheese & wine

cheese

My mother's Lancashire cheese & onion pie

serves 4

for the pastry

60g butter

60g lard

200g self-raising flour

pinch of salt

2–3 tbsp ice-cold water

for the filling

25g butter

3 onions, thinly sliced

1 teacupful of water

salt and plenty of freshly ground white
    pepper (it does not taste quite
    correct, using black)

250–300g Lancashire cheese,
    coarsely grated

a little milk, to both seal and glaze
    the pastry

I have, in the past, written various recipes fashioned around this delicious pie, but I don't think I have ever given the original. Here it is, adapted from her old and slightly battered recipe book, handwritten by Mother. This favourite is one among many others, some having been already handed down by *her* mother. Well, as it always was, in their day.

To make the pastry, cut the butter and lard into small chunks and place in a large bowl with the flour and salt. Gently rub the fat into the flour using fingertips until the texture resembles very coarse breadcrumbs. Mix in only just enough water to bind the mixture together. Lightly knead this dough until well amalgamated, dust with flour and slip into a plastic bag. Place in the fridge for 30 minutes before using.

Preheat the oven to 180°C/350°F/gas mark 4 and also place a flat baking sheet in there, which will help to cook the base of the pie more evenly.

Meanwhile, prepare the filling. Melt the butter in a roomy pan and add the onions. Allow to quietly wilt and stew for about 10 minutes over a gentle heat without colouring. Tip in the water and seasoning and continue to cook over a similar heat, stirring occasionally, until almost all the liquid has been driven off. Decant the onions on to a plate, spread them out and allow to cool.

Lightly butter a loose-bottomed tart tin (approx. 20cm wide x 4cm deep). Roll out two-thirds of the pastry moderately thin and use it to line the base and sides of the tin. Now roll out the remainder to a similar thickness and also generously wide enough to use as a lid for the pie. Cover the base of the pie with half the onions and cover with half the grated cheese. Repeat.

Brush the edges of the pastry case with milk to seal the pastry lid upon it, while also pressing the edges together lightly before trimming off any excess overhang. Brush the surface of the pie with milk. Make 3 small incisions into the centre of the pie using the point of a sharp knife and, if you wish, further decorate the edges of the crust with the tines of a fork.

Put the pie on the preheated baking sheet and bake on the middle shelf of the oven for about 40–50 minutes, or until golden and with a clear indication that tiny oozes of cheese and onion juices are bubbling up through the holes in the middle. Remove from the oven and leave for a good 20–30 minutes before unmoulding and cutting into generous wedges. Best served warm or at room temperature.

poached eggs with Lancashire cheese, leeks & chives

....

serves 4

500g white part of leek, cut into thick
   rings, well washed and drained
350ml water
50g butter
scant ½ tsp ready-ground white pepper
2 tsp Maldon salt

1 bay leaf
250–300g tasty Lancashire cheese,
   coarsely grated
4 large, very fresh eggs
1 tbsp finely snipped chives

....

This recipe produces one of the simplest and nicest dishes. Perfect for a Sunday supper, eaten with thick slices of buttered white bread from a soft and floury bloomer. The eggs should be as fresh as can be, as only then will you achieve a neat and tidy poached egg. I like a splash of vinegar, because I grew up with that flavour, but it also helps to coagulate the white. Generally, I simply crack the eggs into the simmering water, allow them to settle, cover the pan and switch off the heat. Left for 3–4 minutes, they will be runny-yolked and with a just-set white.

Note: use only the white part of the leeks, and try to find large fat ones, for the best flavour, robust and hearty. Also, forgive me, but ready-ground white pepper has the correct taste, here – as it does with cockles in vinegar by the seaside. If you find such a condiment offensive, then please feel free to cook something else.

Put the leeks into a pan with the water, butter, pepper, salt and bay leaf. Bring to the boil, turn down to a low simmer, cover, and cook for about 30 minutes, or until the leeks are good and soft. Heat an overhead grill.

Once the leeks are cooked, stir them well and then divide between 4 preheated shallow, ovenproof dishes. Have a pan of simmering water (add a splash of vinegar, if you like it) ready to poach the eggs. Now sprinkle each dish of leeks with the cheese and place under the grill, only to melt the cheese, not to brown it. Poach the eggs and place one into each dish. Sprinkle over the chives and serve without delay.

risotto alla Parmigiana

....

serves 2

1 small onion, very finely chopped

75g best unsalted butter

400–450ml pale, lightly flavoured
  chicken stock

1 small glass of dry vermouth
  (approx 125ml)

200g carnaroli rice, for preference

3–4 tbsp freshly grated Parmesan

a little salt and freshly ground black pepper

....

The simplest and most daringly naked of all risotti. The dish reminds one that, as always, good risotto-making is all about the rice and how carefully it is cooked. I have, in fact, occasionally made this using only water, where the quality of butter and cheese is even more paramount.

If you find that the rice is cooked before you finish off the stock, don't worry. Conversely, if you think you need more liquid, simply add extra hot water. A good risotto should be of lava-like consistency, lazily oozing, and should take a good few seconds before it finally settles on the plate.

Using a deep-sided, heavy-bottomed pan, quietly fry the onion in 40g of the butter until well softened but not coloured. Meanwhile, heat the stock in another pan. Now add the vermouth to the onions, turn up the heat and reduce until almost evaporated. Pour in the rice and, stirring vigorously using a sturdy wooden spoon, allow the rice to become shiny with butter before adding a ladleful of hot stock. Continuing to stir with vigour, let the rice absorb the stock before adding another ladleful; you may not need all the stock.

When the risotto is looking a lovely, pale ivory colour, is sloppily pourable and the rice is starting to become tender and *not* chalky in the middle (eat the odd grain as you go, to check), remove from the heat and quickly stir in 2 tablespoons of cheese and the remaining butter. Cover and leave to settle for 5 minutes. Now, check for seasoning and vigorously beat the rice together with a wooden spoon until slick and glossy; it should easily fall back on itself when lifted. Spoon on to hot plates and hand around extra Parmesan at table.

Parmesan biscuits

....

makes about 25–30 bicuits

100g cold unsalted butter, cut into chunks

100g plain flour

pinch of salt and cayenne pepper

½ heaped tsp mustard powder

50g finely grated mature Cheddar

50g finely grated Parmesan,
   plus a little extra

1 egg, beaten

....

Those who have come across me before will know that this is a second outing
for these delectable cheese biscuits. However, they are so very good that I felt the
need to force them on you once again, here. My eternal thanks go to my friend
Rachel Cooke, who first showed me how to make them. Ta ever so, Cooky.

Preheat the oven to 180°C/350°F/gas mark 4.

Place the butter and flour in the bowl of a food processor, together with the salt,
cayenne, mustard and cheeses. Process together, to begin with, and then, finally,
pulse the mixture in short spurts as you notice the mixture coming together – as
pastry, if you like. Once the texture is clearly 'clumpy', tip out on to a lightly floured
surface and deftly, but thoroughly, knead it together until well blended and smooth.
Wrap in clingfilm and chill in the fridge for at least 30 minutes.

Lightly flour a work surface and gently roll out the pastry to about 2mm thick.
Cut out the biscuits to the size and shape you wish for – anything between 3cm and
5cm, depending on the occasion. Lay them out on a greased baking tray about 2cm
apart; it may take two lots of baking to use up the entire mixture. Carefully brush
the surface of each biscuit with the egg and sprinkle over a little finely grated
Parmesan. Bake in the oven for 10 minutes, or until a gorgeous golden colour
is achieved; the superb smell will also inform you that they are ready. Carefully
lift off the tray using a palette knife and place on a rack to cool. Although the
biscuits will keep well in a sealed container for a few days, I have never known
this to happen.

Roquefort, pear & chicory salad with walnut oil

....

serves 2

2–3 heads of chicory, separated into
   leaves and put to soak in iced water
100–125g Roquefort, crumbled
1 large, ripe pear, peeled and thinly sliced

a squeeze of lemon juice
2–3 tbsp walnut oil
freshly ground black pepper

....

Of all blue cheeses, Roquefort will always remain my favourite. I will take
a small slice of Stilton – or even better, Stichelton – at Christmas, or maybe
a thick wedge of sweetly savoury Fourme d'Ambert when in a good French
restaurant. And I am very fond of a fine and creamy Gorgonzola or Dolcelatte,
from time to time. But Roquefort, the king of blue cheeses, takes the biscuit.

    Anyway, here is a very fine, very simple salad: all at once fresh, crisp, salty,
sweet and fragrantly oily – and just perfect when using Roquefort that is cool
and crumbly. Use either the red-leafed or traditional white chicory, here.

Dry the chicory leaves (a spinner is best, here) and neatly arrange on a serving dish,
inner curved sides uppermost. Evenly distribute the pear in and among the leaves,
crumble over the cheese and squeeze over a touch of lemon juice. Trickle over the
walnut oil and grind over the pepper. Serve forthwith.

Roquefort tart

serves 6, as a first course

pastry (see page 170)

25g butter

250g leeks, well trimmed, sliced, washed and drained

2 egg yolks

2 eggs

150ml double cream

100ml soured cream

small bunch of chives, finely chopped

a little salt and plenty of freshly ground black pepper

freshly grated nutmeg

250g Roquefort, cut into small chunks

Once again, the combination of cheese and allium knows no boundaries. The texture here should be wobbling and luscious, and with a crisp pastry shell holding everything together – but only just ... Other firm blue cheeses may be used instead, but the deeply savoury and complex Roquefort, once again, shines through.

For the pastry, please refer to the Quiche Lorraine (see page 170). You may not need all of it, so freeze the remainder, wrapped in clingfilm.

Preheat the oven to 180°C/350°F/gas mark 4. Place a flat baking sheet in the oven, too, to help the cooking of the base of the pastry case.

Roll out the pastry as thinly as possible and line a 20cm wide by 4cm deep tart tin. Lightly prick the base of the pastry with a fork all over, and then bake blind. This is done by lining the uncooked pastry case with a sheet of kitchen foil and filling with some dried haricot beans, for instance. It is then cooked on the flat baking sheet for about 15–20 minutes, removed from the oven, the foil and beans transferred to a container for future use. Return to the oven for a further 10 minutes or so, until it is pale golden, crisp and well cooked through, particularly the base.

Now, melt the butter in a pan and add the leeks. Allow to quietly stew until soft, and with very little bubbling buttery juices left in the pan. Tip out on to a plate and leave until cool. Loosely whisk together the egg yolks and whole eggs in a bowl. Stir in both the creams, the chives, a little salt, pepper and nutmeg and set aside.

Strew the leeks over the base of the tart case and then cover these with the nuggets of Roquefort, evenly distributed. Pour over two-thirds of the egg/cream mixture and slide the tart into the oven. Only now add the remaining mixture as high as you dare, therefore avoiding spillage caused by shaky transportation. Bake for about 40–50 minutes, or until lightly puffed and set, with a gorgeous golden surface. Serve warm, not hot.

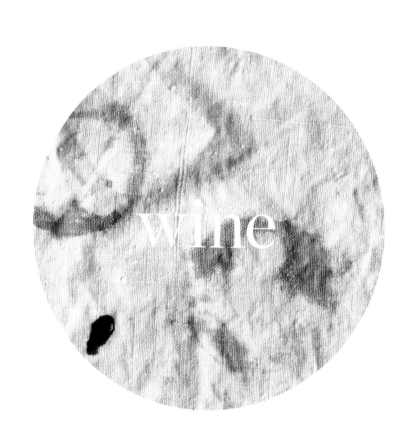

pork chops with white wine, mustard & cheese

....

serves 4

1 tbsp olive oil

salt and freshly ground black pepper

4 thick pork chops, rind removed

200ml dry white wine

75g grated Gruyère or Emmenthal

1 level tbsp drained, rinsed and lightly
    crushed soft green peppercorns
    (from a jar or tin)

125ml double cream

1 heaped tbsp Dijon mustard

approx. 10 sage leaves, torn up into pieces

....

A rich and winy sort of assembly, here, that would be very good eating on
a wet and wintry night. There is also something of a Swiss-chalet flavour
about it, too, after a day out in the snow. A very nice accompaniment would
be a side dish of big fat gherkins, which further affords a pleasing contrast
to the lavish dairy notes of the dish.

Preheat an overhead grill.

Heat the olive oil in a large, heavy-bottomed frying pan. Season the chops and fry
on both sides until golden. Tip off any excess oil, turn down the heat a little and
pour in the wine. Allow to bubble and then reduce the heat to low, so that the wine
simmers gently and reduces by about half. Turn the chops once again during this
process, which should amount to about 10 minutes' cooking time in all.

Meanwhile, mix together the cheese, peppercorns, cream, mustard and sage in a
small bowl. Spread this paste on to the cooked chops and place the whole assembly
under the grill, until all has bubbled and melted to a golden finish.

Remove the chops to a hot serving dish, then take the pan and place it back on a low
heat; some of the mixture will have slipped off the chops into the winy juices, so
just whisk it in. Gently reheat this 'sauce' and pour it around the chops. Plainly
boiled potatoes are best, here, I think.

coq au vin

serves 4

1 bottle of decent red wine,
  preferably Pinot Noir
1 dsp redcurrant jelly
1 small onion, chopped
2 sticks of celery, chopped
1 carrot, chopped
4 cloves of garlic, unpeeled
  and bruised
3–4 sprigs of thyme
2 bay leaves
2 cloves

4 large chicken joints: drumstick
  and thigh, skin removed
1 tbsp olive oil
25g butter
100g smoked pancetta, in a piece,
  rind removed, cut into large cubes
salt and freshly ground black pepper
1 tbsp flour
20 button onions, peeled (cover with
  boiling water for a couple of
  minutes to ease peeling)
20 button mushrooms
3 tbsp Cognac

The first time I made coq au vin, aged about sixteen, it turned out as a bit of a purple, watery mess. The wine was cheap (I think Dad may have gone down the Hirondelle route, assuming you may recall that particular vinous delight), with the taste insipid as a result. The bacon – well … it was just any old bacon, probably. The chicken itself, then, was probably quite a good one, but I had overcooked it so much, the breast parts turned to rags. Mum, bless her, thought the mushrooms were the best part. 'Nice and juicy,' she said. I certainly remember that bit.

You may be pleased to know I'm better at it now. So, read on … Try not to miss out the preliminary cooking of the wine, together with its useful aromatics.

Put the first 9 ingredients into a stainless steel or enamelled pot and bring to the boil. Leave over a medium flame until reduced by one third. Strain through a fine sieve and cool completely. Marinate the chicken pieces in this for at least 5–6 hours or, preferably, overnight.

Warm the olive oil and butter in a solid-bottomed pot or frying pan and gently fry the pancetta until golden. Remove with a slotted spoon and reserve. Season the chicken joints and roll in the flour, then fry until golden brown in the olive oil/fat remaining from the pancetta. Remove these, too, and put with the reserved pancetta.

Now tip the onions and mushrooms into the pot and gently cook until well coloured – about 10 minutes. Tip out all the fat, return the chicken and bacon to the pot, turn up the heat and pour over the Cognac. Set alight, allow the flames to die down and then add the reserved, reduced wine. Shake about a bit, allowing everything to settle down, then cover and put on a very low heat. Simmer at a merest 'blip', partially covered, for about 1 hour. Alternatively, use an oven preheated to 170°C/325°F/gas mark 3.

Serve the coq au vin with simply boiled or steamed potatoes, lubricated with melted butter. You may also like to garnish the dish in a classical manner, by frying some little bread triangles, dipping their edges in some of the red wine sauce, and then in chopped parsley.

Note: a good coq au vin tastes infinitely better reheated the next day. This also allows for any fat that has collected on the surface to be easily removed, having solidified in the fridge.

poached eggs in coq au vin gravy

serves 1
2 very fresh eggs, poached (see page 57)
some reserved sauce and pancetta
 from leftover coq au vin
chopped parsley

And here is a delicious way to use up leftover sauce from a coq au vin. If there is not enough pancetta left, cook a bit more, but don't bother to add any mushrooms or onions; this is all about eggs, bacon and red wine. You may also like to do the croutons here, too (see opposite). Just pop one under each egg and omit the dippy-parsley thing; just sprinkle some over the eggs.

Incidentally, if you have ever read Edouard de Pomiane's *Cooking in Ten Minutes,* you will understand how very nice a dainty little dish such as this can be.

Put the freshly poached eggs into a small, heated dish. Heat up some of the sauce and pancetta from leftover coq au vin. Pour over the eggs and garnish with chopped parsley. Eat at once.

baked trout with Chablis, cream & tarragon

....

serves 2

50g softened butter

2–3 shallots, sliced

2 trout

5–6 sprigs of tarragon

salt and freshly ground black pepper

250ml Chablis

200ml whipping cream

squeeze of lemon juice, to taste

....

An underrated little fish is the trout. Yes, it may now be farmed, but it is generally as fresh as a daisy because of this. Long gone are regular supplies of wild brown trout from British rivers, more is the pity. But also, pity not the delicacy that a carefully farmed fish will give to the following, traditional French preparation.

Preheat the oven to 200ºC/400ºF/gas mark 6.

Using half the butter, grease a baking dish (preferably oval and nice enough to present at table) that will accommodate the trout fairly snugly. Sprinkle the base of the dish with the shallots, then smear the remaining butter over the fish and lay them in the dish. Tuck in 3 or 4 sprigs of tarragon (keep the remainder for later), torn up a bit, and season the trout inside and out. Pour over the Chablis, then tightly cover with kitchen foil and bake in the oven for 20 minutes. Remove from the oven, foil intact, and leave to rest for a further 10 minutes.

Now, lift off the foil and invert it on to a large plate. Flick off any clinging bits of shallot from the trout and carefully lift them onto the foil. Transfer everything left in the baking dish to a saucepan, and clean the dish. Remove the skin and heads from the fish with a small knife and add them to the saucepan. Return the skinned trout to the baking dish and re-cover with foil. Keep warm while you make the sauce.

Set the saucepan over a moderate heat and allow the sauce to reduce until nearly all the liquid has been driven off and the mixture is syrupy. Add the cream and stir together. Bring to a simmer and cook gently for 20 minutes or so, until the sauce is a nice ivory colour.

Strain through a fine sieve into another pan, pushing down hard on the solids to extract every last vestige of flavour. Taste for seasoning, add a touch of lemon juice and add the leaves from the remaining tarragon, finely chopped. Pour the sauce over the trout and serve with plainly boiled, buttered potatoes.

oily
vegetables

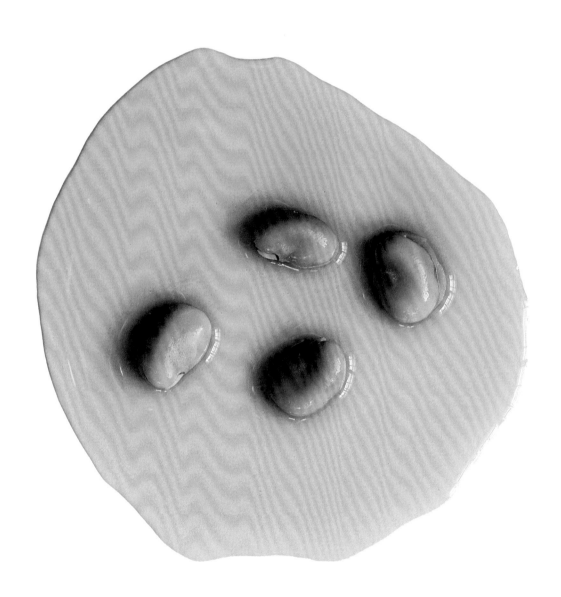

Tuscan tomato & bread salad (panzanella)

serves about 8

As with a salade niçoise (see page 21), the assembly for this Italian bread salad is a little bit about taste and balance, both for the maker and for those who enjoy to eat it. So, with this in mind, it would be far better to talk through the recipe rather than give a list of exact ingredients and amounts.

I have made and eaten plenty of panzanella salads, in the UK and in Italy, too – and once in California, which was, I happily admit, possibly the best of all; it was the tomatoes that were so very good. And that, apart from the bread, is what this salad is all about. There really is no point in making it unless the tomatoes are of fine quality and ripe, ripe, ripe. Some insist that the only ingredients for a panzanella are bread and tomatoes, with just a sprightly seasoning of garlic, basil, vinegar and olive oil and nothing else. The simple Tuscan bread and tomato soup, 'pappa pomodoro', comes to mind as a sloppy, warm version of this salad's ingredients, in fact. The region, certainly, is common to both.

Both these dishes rely on bread – and leftover bread, at that. No self-respecting cook would make either the salad or the soup with an especially purchased loaf. Each is a peasant assembly; a seasonally filling dish for when there is a regular stale ingredient mixed with a seasonal glut of the other. This, however, does not mean that a panzanella salad cannot be a gastronomic treat. Just don't be tempted to fuss too much over the thing.

Personally, I love *cucumber* in mine, as well as some thinly sliced *red onions* (the only time I ever use them), preferring sweet white onions most of the time. I peel my cucumber because I find the skin intrusive, here (use the skin in a pre-lunch Pimm's, as it is here that it is most useful, strong and pretty in the glass). Cut the cucumber into small chunks, not dice, and set aside in a large, deep serving bowl with a little *salt*. Pile the onions on top, together with plenty of *pepper*. Think one medium cucumber to one small onion, as a rough ratio. Now, for the staples ...

As with cucumber, I like to slip the skins off the *tomatoes* (pop in boiling water for a few seconds), then cut them into slightly larger pieces than the cucumber. Allow about double the weight of tomatoes to cucumber. Cover the cucumber and onion in the bowl with the tomatoes, scatter over about 3 finely chopped *cloves of garlic* and add a little more *salt*. Mix everything together – hands are best, here, and it is quite a pleasure to do. Add a couple of tablespoons of *red wine vinegar*, about 6–7 of fine and fruity *olive oil*, and leave to macerate for 30 minutes.

Meanwhile, deal with the *bread*. It should be broken up into chunks of random size. Well, 'should', here, is moot; their size and shape will be determined by how stale the bread and how strong one's fingers, and random will not be a matter of choice. In terms of quantity, allow about 4–5 handfuls of bread chunks. Thoroughly mix into the macerated salad (a good deal of juice will have formed), together with the leaves from a large bunch of *basil*, torn into pieces. Try not to leave longer than about 10 minutes before eating, so that the bread retains an inner crunch. Maybe not traditional Tuscan, but this is the way I like my panzanella.

salad of broad beans, smoked cod's roe, ricotta & olive oil

....

serves 4

2kg broad beans, podded

200g fresh ricotta

125–150g firm smoked cod's roe,
   peeled of its membrane

fine and fruity olive oil

salt and freshly ground black pepper

....

Truthfully, this is nothing more than an assembly of immaculate ingredients. However, it is an harmonious and sunny sort of thing, with its green slippery beans, splashes of bright white cheese and golden-orange roe, all glistening with fruity olive oil. If you can get it, there lurks some astonishingly delicious sheep's milk ricotta in occasional fine cheese shops. Enquire of your favourite monger for this rare, fermented curd.

Before you start, have ready a bowl of cold water with several ice cubes in it.

Cook the broad beans in boiling salted water for about a minute. Drain and immediately plunge them into the bowl of ice-cold water. Peel the pale green skins off the beans and put on a shallow serving dish. Randomly place pieces of ricotta and thin slivers of the roe over the beans, then liberally douse with olive oil. Season with salt and pepper.

Eat with bread.

wilted greens wrapped in Parma ham

serves 4

12 slices of Parma ham

for the dressing
good pinch of sea salt
1 small clove of garlic, crushed to a
   paste with the above
2 tbsp red wine vinegar
1 small shallot, very finely chopped
freshly ground black pepper
5–6 tbsp olive oil

for the greens, all well washed and dried
2 large handfuls of small spinach leaves
2 large handfuls of watercress
2 large handfuls of pea shoots
1 large handful of rocket
several mint leaves, roughly chopped

I ought to say here that when it comes to the most beautiful Parma ham, I cannot think of anything more than just that; quite unadorned and fiddled about with, laid upon a pristine white plate in delicately rumpled sheets. However, sometimes, just sometimes, it is interesting to see how a judicious and tasteful addition can work with an ingredient that is, how shall we say, happy in itself.

We used to serve a version of this at Bibendum, some years ago now. I think it is rather nice. For one thing, although it is a composed dish, both components shine without outdoing the other: the greens quietly warm the ham, while their wrapping offers a meaty note of great subtlety and savour. A swish dish.

Make the dressing by whisking together the first 5 ingredients, then slowly incorporate the olive oil as for making a vinaigrette dressing – which is, after all, what it is. Pour into a wok or large frying pan and begin to warm it over a low heat. Tip in all the greens and toss and turn using a couple of salad servers, say, until wilted but not limp past recovery. Pile into a colander set over a large bowl, reserving the precious liquid beneath. Allow the greens to cool to a warm, room temperature. Once well drained, pour the 'precious liquid' into a small, stainless steel pan and reduce, over a moderate heat, until well flavoured and with the look of a murky-looking dressing; the greens will have imparted their stain but also, more importantly, their flavour to the original, simple vinaigrette. Add this reduced liquid back to the drained greens.

Now, put a tablespoon of the greens on a slice of ham, deftly roll it up and place on a large flat serving dish. Repeat this process with the remaining 11 slices of ham, so arranging them that they will please the eye. Spoon the reduced dressing over these diminutive bundles and serve forthwith.

I have been known to fling an occasional dusting of freshly grated Parmesan over these, from time to time. Feel free, but don't go mad.

Piedmontese peppers

serves 4

4 red peppers

8–12 ripe plum tomatoes

4 cloves of garlic, peeled

a little salt

freshly ground black pepper

5–6 tbsp good olive oil

8 large Spanish tinned anchovies,
cut in half lengthways,
or 16 whole small ones

In the early 1990s, pictures of this dish adorned the tiled walls alongside the escalators on the Bakerloo line. They were extracted from an excellent, best-selling cookery book of the time. However, it was a bit surreal to see a plate of food, originally from a recipe in Elizabeth David's *Italian Food*, now illustrated on London's ancient tube system. Then again, it was good to see such a pretty picture at rush hour. And, furthermore, it may have inspired the occasional commuter to rush home and cook such a thing. Without beating about the bush, it is the most delicious event ever to happen to a pepper.

Preheat the oven to 190°C/375°F/gas mark 5. Cut the red peppers in half, lengthways, slicing right through the stalk (leave it attached, simply for the look of the finished dish). Remove the seeds and cut out the pithy parts. Pour boiling water over the plum tomatoes, leave for 10 seconds, peel off their skins and then cut out the core. Place the halved peppers into an ovenproof dish (one that will be nice enough to present later, at table). Slice the garlic into slivers, distribute over the inside of the peppers and then fit the tomatoes inside, pushing them gently into the space. Add only a little salt, but a normal grinding of pepper. Spoon over the olive oil and then slide the dish into the oven. Bake for about 45 minutes to 1 hour, turning the heat down a little if you notice any excessive scorching of the peppers.

Once they are nicely softened, slightly collapsed, scorched in places and smelling quite wonderful (they always do), remove from the oven. Criss-cross each pepper half with an anchovy, baste with the copious, oily juices and allow to cool to room temperature.

gazpacho

....

serves 6

75ml sherry vinegar

300ml water

1 cucumber, peeled and chopped

1 red pepper, seeded and chopped

1 green pepper, seeded and chopped

500g very ripe tomatoes, skinned
   and chopped

150ml passata

3 cloves of garlic, peeled and crushed

1 onion, chopped

1 scant tsp Tabasco

small handful of mint leaves

salt and freshly ground black pepper

400g crushed ice

200ml extra virgin olive oil

to serve

tiny croutons, made from a few slices
      of white bread, cubed, and then fried
      in olive oil until crisp

....

Hot Spanish sunshine. Chilled glass of fino. Lunch. 2.30pm. Post swim. T-shirt and damp shorts. Espadrilles. Panama hat. Unfed cat at sandy feet. Beachside table. More hot Spanish sunshine. Cold soup. Gazpacho.

Note: there are those who think that a gazpacho should be chunky or garnished with more of the already included ingredients as dice. I don't. I love the smoothness of this recipe and find that bits of extra vegetables simply get in the way. However, I wouldn't miss out on the croutons for anything. I have said many times before that croutons in any smooth soup – hot or cold – do lovely things to the mouth, when supping.

Purée all the soup ingredients together until smooth, apart from about a third of the olive oil. Pass through an ordinary, round sieve (not too fine) while pressing down well on the vegetables to extract as much flavour as possible. Whisk in the rest of the olive oil and pour into chilled soup bowls; although the soup is already chilled due to the crushed ice, drop an extra ice cube into each serving. Hand round croutons at table.

a mix of mushrooms, pasta, garlic & parsley

baked pappardelle with pancetta & porcini

....

serves 2, heartily

500ml milk
20g dried porcini
40g butter
25g plain flour
salt and freshly ground black pepper

100g pappardelle
50g thinly sliced pancetta,
   cut into 2cm pieces
4–5 tbsp freshly grated Parmesan

....

The following, utterly delicious recipe has been inspired by two of my most loved restaurants. The first one, that venerable Venetian institution, Harry's Bar, makes a gratin of fine ribbon pasta (tagliolini), which is baked with slivers of smoked ham in a rich béchamel sauce, then finished with a fine crust of Parmesan.

The other place is the Walnut Tree Inn, near Abergavenny, when Franco Taruschio used to run it as chef-proprietor together with his wife, Ann, for over three decades. The dish in question here was the legendary Vincisgrassi: fresh porcini (often picked locally) and Parma ham, layered between sheets of lasagne and thick smears of béchamel, also baked with Parmesan. Franco's extra joy was to shave a generous topping of white truffle on the finished dish, just before sending to table. The smell, oh, the smell! – as it was placed before this greedy boy.

Preheat the oven to 200°C/400°F/gas mark 6.

Just warm the milk in a saucepan and then soak the porcini in it for about 10 minutes. Drain the milk through a sieve suspended over a bowl, pressing lightly on the porcini with the back of a ladle to extract all the milk. Put the mushrooms to one side. Rinse out the pan and wipe it clean, then use it to melt the butter. Tip in the flour, stir it around and cook quietly for a few minutes without colouring the roux. Pour in the porcini-flavoured milk all in one go and whisk together vigorously until smooth. Cook over a very low heat, stirring now with a wooden spoon, for about 10 minutes, until the sauce has thickened – and it should not be too thick. Season lightly with salt and generously with pepper. Put on a lid and set aside.

Bring a large pan of boiling, salted water to a rolling boil. Plunge in the pasta, bring back to the boil and cook until it is a little underdone (taste some); it will cook more when it is baked. Drain in a colander, tip into a roomy bowl and deftly mix with the sauce, while also introducing the porcini and pieces of pancetta. Once well amalgamated, tip into a lightly buttered dish and lightly tap down. Strew about 2 tablespoons of Parmesan over the surface and bake in the oven for 30–40 minutes, or until it is bubbling around the edges and the top is gorgeously crusted a light brown. Take to table in its dish and spoon out on to hot plates, the remaining cheese handed separately to sprinkle over each serving.

mushroom broth with tarragon cream

serves 4

2 large onions, coarsely chopped

2–3 tbsp olive oil

a small slice of butter

750g flat, dark-gilled mushrooms,
   coarsely chopped

2 cloves of garlic, crushed

salt and freshly ground black pepper

125ml dry vermouth

1½ litres light chicken stock

5–6 sprigs of tarragon, tied into
   a bundle with string

2 tbsp Madeira

for the tarragon cream

150ml double cream

a touch of salt and freshly ground
   black pepper

1 tsp tarragon vinegar

4–5 sprigs of tarragon, leaves only,
   finely chopped

The flavour of mushroom with tarragon is a happy one. I particularly enjoy this limpid, ever so tasty broth when the dollop of tarragon-scented cream melts into it in the most agreeable manner.

Note: if a mushroom cream soup is made in the more usual way, by adding cream to the finished soup and blending to a smooth finish, this can be very delicious, too. If you were to take this route, add the tarragon cream to the blender once the mushroom broth has been liquidised to a smooth finish. Process for just a few seconds, then pass through a fine sieve into a bowl. This is particularly nice chilled, decanted into cold soup bowls and eaten out of doors as a first course to a sunny weekend lunch.

Fry the onions in the olive oil and butter until softened. Add the mushrooms, with a little more oil if necessary, and cook both ingredients until golden brown. Add the garlic and seasoning, turn up the heat and stir-fry for a couple of minutes. Add the vermouth, allow to bubble vigorously, then pour in the stock and add the bundle of tarragon. Cover and simmer gently for 40 minutes. Strain through a colander into a clean pan and leave to settle for a few minutes; now is the time to remove any excess fat from the surface of the broth with sheets of kitchen paper.

Remove the tarragon bundle from the mushroom mulch and discard. Now tip this mulch into the bowl of a food processor and pulse until the mixture is nicely coarse. Add back to the broth, check the seasoning and pour in the Madeira. Keep warm.

To make the tarragon cream, simply whisk everything together until lightly thickened, taking care not to over-beat the assembly; the vinegar will begin to thicken the mixture the minute it is added, anyway.

Bring the soup back to a simmer, pour into heated, deep soup bowls and add a spoonful of cream to each serving.

mushrooms with garlic, parsley & lemon, with olive oil & potato purée

serves 4

for the potato purée

1kg waxy potatoes, peeled and
   cut into chunks

salt

2 large cloves of garlic, peeled and halved

75–100ml milk

125–150ml fine olive oil

pinch of cayenne pepper

for the mushrooms

400g medium open-cup mushrooms, sliced

2 tbsp olive oil

small bunch of flat-leaf parsley,
   leaves only, chopped

3 cloves of garlic

zest of 1 small lemon

salt and freshly ground black pepper

2 tbsp double cream (optional)

to serve

a little extra fine olive oil and
   chopped parsley

lemon (optional)

I can only look upon this as the perfect, impromptu supper dish, especially when most of the ingredients are usually to hand; mushrooms, in my kitchen at least, are often to be found languishing in the salad drawer of the fridge, usually soon after I have found one of those large packets of super-value mushrooms at my local supermarket. Potatoes and parsley, I pretty well always have lurking about. The remaining ingredients are never out of stock.

I love the common or garden cultivated mushroom, and it is so versatile and delicious when treated in the following way, partnered with its most favourite flavours of garlic and parsley. The lemon zest adds a further fragrance to the dish, which is pleasing. And the potato is the most delectable partner, soaking up the juices as a gorgeously smooth mattress.

Boil the potatoes in salted water with the garlic until tender. Warm the milk in a small pan. Drain the potatoes and garlic well. Using either a potato ricer (best), or a mouli-légumes, purée the potatoes/garlic into a bowl. Now, alternately, whisk in the milk and olive oil in thin streams until a slightly sloppier than usual puréed potato mixture is achieved, then spike with a pinch of cayenne. Keep warm, covered with kitchen foil, over a pan of barely simmering water.

Fry the mushrooms in the olive oil until pale golden. Finely chop the parsley, garlic and lemon zest together (the scent from doing this is just wonderful). Add this to the mushrooms with a little seasoning, turn up the heat a little and stir-fry until well mixed together. If you would like to 'cream' the mushrooms, stir in the double cream now, and allow to bubble for a minute or two.

To serve, spoon the potato purée into 4 hot shallow soup plates and divide the mushrooms between each of them. Trickle over a touch more olive oil and scatter with parsley. Offer some pieces of lemon at table for those who may enjoy a sharp, finishing touch to the dish.

smoky salty fish

homemade gravadlax with cucumber salad & mustard sauce

....

serves 4

for the salmon

85g caster sugar

70g sea salt

2 tbsp schnapps, gin, vodka or similar

10g freshly ground white pepper

10g freeze-dried dill, or a 100g bunch
   of fresh dill, stalks and all

500g boneless, skinless salmon fillet

for the cucumber salad

1 large cucumber, peeled and thinly sliced

1 tsp sea salt

2 tsp caster sugar

freshly ground white pepper

1–2 tbsp white wine vinegar, or to taste

for the sauce

3 tbsp smooth Dijon mustard

a good squeeze of lemon juice, to taste

2 tsp caster sugar

2–3 tbsp salad oil, say sunflower

1–2 tsp freeze-dried dill, or 1 tbsp
   freshly chopped dill (sprigs only, this time)

salt and freshly ground white pepper

....

The obvious question to ask is this: why would one ever wish to make gravadlax when it is now almost as easy to buy as smoked salmon – and who would bother to make that?

Well ... as with freshly sliced smoked salmon from a whole side (which knocks spots off pre-sliced and vacuum-packed fish), however fine the original quality of the cure and smoke, pre-slicing and vacuum-packing unnaturally compresses the flesh. And the same problem clearly applies to packets of salmon cured to make gravadlax. The answer is, make your own and slice your own. And I can't think of a simpler recipe than the one that follows.

To cure the salmon, put the first 5 ingredients into a small food processor and work together to a sloppy green paste. Place half of this in a container (a plastic box with a lid, say) that will accommodate the fish snugly. Lay the salmon on top of this, press it down, then cover with the other half of the mixture, smearing it well over the surface of the fish. Pop on the lid, place in the fridge, and leave there for 48 hours, turning the fish occasionally, until firm to the touch. Carefully rinse the fish, but not so much that no remnants of dill remain adhered. Dry with kitchen paper, wrap in clingfilm and keep cold in the fridge.

To make the cucumber salad, mix together all the ingredients in a bowl and leave to macerate for about an hour. Drain off the liquid, put the cucumber in a serving dish and keep cool in the fridge. For the sauce, whisk together the mustard, lemon juice and sugar, then whisk in the oil until you have a loose, thick dressing. Stir in the dill and adjust the seasoning, if necessary. Pour into a small serving bowl.

To serve, thinly slice the gravadlax at an angle and present on a large serving dish. Hand both the cucumber salad and mustard sauce at table.

salt cod baked with potatoes & olive oil

serves 2, generously

300g piece of salt cod, soaked in
   several changes of cold water, for at
   least 24 hours

300ml milk

3 cloves of garlic, finely chopped

2–3 small dried red chillies,
   broken up a little

500g waxy potatoes, peeled and
   cut into thick matchsticks

2–3 tbsp double cream

2–3 tbsp fine olive oil

3–4 tbsp fresh white breadcrumbs

several flecks of butter

I was inspired to create this dish (not many of those left to us cooks) by the great Swedish potato recipe for something called 'Jansson's Temptation'. Here, Swedish anchovies (cured and marinated sprats, in fact) are buried within a great big dish of thick potato matchsticks – for want of a better description – chopped onions and plenty of cream. The surface is finally topped with breadcrumbs and butter before being baked to a golden-crusted, bubbling mass. Talk about rich – but very, very delicious it most surely is.

Here, some less rich milk is used as the main dairy ingredient and garlic replaces the onions; salt cod and garlic are never far away from each other at the best of times. And although a touch of cream is added at the last minute, it is the olive oil – together with the garlic, naturally – which transports the dish from the cold, Scandinavian north, to the sunnier climes of the South of France.

Preheat the oven to 180°C/350°F/gas mark 4.

Put the cod into a saucepan and cover it with the milk. Simmer ever so gently for about 10 minutes. Drain through a sieve suspended over a bowl, keeping the milk beneath. Allow the fish to cool, carefully remove any bones and skin, then flake it into pieces. Return the fish to the bowl of milk, together with the garlic, chillies, potatoes and cream. Mix well. Take a deep oven dish (one that will also look good from which to serve), fill it with the fish mixture and spoon over the olive oil, while also slightly mixing it into the liquid, so that it appears as occasional pools. Strew the breadcrumbs liberally over the entire surface, dot with flakes of butter, then slide into the oven. Bake for about 40 minutes, or until the breadcrumbs are golden and nicely crusted.

smoked haddock pilaf with ginger & coriander

....

serves 2, as a light lunch or supper dish

40g butter

2 tsp garam masala

250g basmati rice
   (Tilda brand, for preference)

375ml light chicken stock

1 bay leaf

grated zest of 1 small lemon

2 mild green chillies, seeded and chopped

a small knob of fresh ginger, peeled
   and finely grated

a little salt and freshly ground black pepper

400g undyed smoked haddock fillet,
   boned and skinned, cut into 2 equal
   pieces

2 hard-boiled eggs, chopped

2 spring onions, trimmed and finely sliced

1 tbsp chopped coriander

lemon juice, to taste

....

A good pilaf is a wondrous thing, for me. This is partly to do with having trouble cooking rice successfully for years – decades, even – but also because when a pilaf works really well, it remains possibly my favourite way to eat rice in any form (a risotto comes in at a very close second, but only just).

The important thing is never to mistrust the following ratio of rice to liquid. This is correct. My friend, the photographer Jason Lowe (whose superb illustrations grace this book) once cooked a lamb pilaf recipe I gave him, only to lose faith at the last minute, adding a touch more liquid to the pot. Result? Stodgy pilaf. He won't be doing that again in a hurry – he is, in fact, a naturally instinctive, very good cook indeed (if that does not sound too patronising).

For preference, I always use Tilda basmati rice, and never, ever wash it. This goes against many opinions of my peers, but it works perfectly for me every time.

Preheat the oven to 180°C/350°F/gas mark 4.

Melt the butter in a solid-bottomed, lidded ovenproof cooking pot. Add the garam masala and allow to sizzle gently for a moment or two. Tip in the rice and stir around until the grains are well coated with this spicy butter. Pour in the stock and add the bay leaf, lemon zest, green chillies, ginger and a touch of seasoning. Bring up to a simmer, then slip in the haddock fillets, gently submerging them under the surface. Put on the lid and slide the pot into the oven. Cook for 20 minutes.

Remove from the oven, then leave to stand for 5–7 minutes without removing the lid; this is important, allowing the rice to finish cooking. Take off the lid, immediately tip in the chopped egg, onions and coriander and, using 2 forks, gently mix the rice about, while also breaking the fish into flakes and mixing everything else in as you go. Remove the bay leaf, then cover the pot with a tea-towel, clamp on the lid, and leave for a further 5 minutes, so allowing excess steam to evaporate. Serve directly from the pot on to hot plates and squeeze over a little lemon juice.

smoked haddock & spinach, with chive butter sauce

....

serves 4

4 pieces of smoked haddock,
    approx. 150–175g each,
    boned and skinned

275ml milk

for the hollandaise sauce

3 egg yolks

200g unsalted butter, melted

a little salt and generous freshly
    ground white pepper

juice of ½ a lemon

2 tbsp snipped chives

for the spinach

500g spinach leaves

25g butter

salt and freshly ground black pepper

....

A simple-sounding little dish, but I hope you won't mind having a go at
the hollandaise sauce, which is integral to the success of the assembly.
The method for the sauce is a traditional one, but you may like to go down
the small food processor route, which is a good deal easier. In this case, the
texture emerges slightly different from the original (more emulsified), but
as it is thinned down with the haddock-cooking milk later, this is not the
end of the world, culinary-wise.

To do this quick method, simply place the egg yolks in a small food processor
with a splash of water, switch on and process until airy and pale. Heat the butter
until quite hot and bubbling (use a small pan with a lip, to aid pouring) and, with
the motor running, slowly pour in the butter until the sauce has become thick,
as with making mayonnaise. You may like to add a touch of the melted butter's
milky residue, as the processor method usually makes a much thicker sauce.
Season as explained overleaf.

To make the hollandaise sauce, whisk together the egg yolks with a tiny splash of water in a stainless steel pan over a very low heat, until thick and smooth. Now, off the heat, continue to whisk while pouring in the melted butter in a thin stream, leaving behind the milky residue that has settled in the bottom of the butter pan. Season the sauce and sharpen with lemon juice, to taste. Keep warm.

To cook the smoked haddock, very gently poach the pieces in the milk on a low simmer for 2 minutes. Leave in the milk while you quickly prepare the spinach. Cook this in a large frying pan in the butter with a little seasoning, until wilted and glossy. Drain in a colander to remove excess liquid, then divide the spinach between 4 warmed plates. Fish out the 4 pieces of haddock from the milk, drain for a moment on kitchen paper, then place one on top of each plate of spinach.

For the sauce, loosen the hollandaise with a little of the poaching milk and whisk to a pouring consistency. Stir in the chives and spoon over the fish and spinach. Serve forthwith.

marinated sardine fillets

....

serves 4, as a first course

approx. 700g very fresh, large sardines
   (Cornish pilchards, usually),
   filleted, or use similar-sized herrings

50g sea salt

juice of 1 large lemon

1 medium onion, peeled and thinly sliced

a few black peppercorns, sprigs of fresh
   thyme, crumbled dried red chillies,
   a bay leaf or two ...

7–8 tbsp fruity olive oil

....

The instruction 'Ask your fishmonger to fillet and bone the fish for you' fills me with fear and trepidation these days. I mean, just how many skilled fishmongers are there left? I recently saw a clutch of magazine recipes where the reader was instructed to ask his monger to de-beard his big bag of mussels ... I imagine the muttered reply to this request would be, how shall we say, mostly unprintable, here.

Anyway, it *is* possible to do it yourself, with trial and error, but a truly dedicated fishmonger will be more than happy to, especially if you are a regular customer. Just give him some notice, is all I ask. The occasional supermarket fishmonger may also be able to help.

Put the fish fillets into a rectangular dish and strew with the salt. Cover, and put in the fridge for 24 hours, turning them once. Lift out the fillets, throw away the exuded, salty juices, rinse them and pat dry. Now, put the fillets into a plastic box that has a lid. Squeeze over the lemon juice, cover with the onions and scatter with the peppercorns, thyme, chillies, bay, etc. Spoon over the olive oil, put on the lid and place in a very cool place for 24 hours – preferably not in the fridge, unless the weather is more than clement. Remove to room temperature 1 hour before serving, decant on to a pretty serving dish, and eat with brown bread and butter. For a light lunch or supper dish, serve up with a bowl of hot, buttered new potatoes.

small dishes of kipper & tomato baked in cream

serves 2, for a light supper,
   or as a weekend breakfast treat
1 undyed kipper
a little soft butter
6 or 7 small to medium plum tomatoes
4–5 tbsp double cream

2 tsp English-made mustard
   (Colman's, preferably)
a couple of pinches of curry powder
a touch of salt, if necessary

For the best flavour, here, use a whole, undyed kipper as instructed. However, if you are less than bold with bones, buy kipper fillets. The boiling water step remains the same for filleted fish, even though they may look just a little bit underdone in the middle, as the fish will continue to cook a little more, once in the oven. 'A sweet dish with great charm,' a kind friend once said when I served it up to him.

Preheat the oven to 200°C/400°F/gas mark 6.

Put the kipper into a shallow dish. Boil a kettle and submerge the kipper in the boiling water. Leave there for 5 minutes, and drain. Leave to cool for a few minutes, then flake off most of the meat that is not too riddled with whiskery bones. Pile the kipper meat into the centre of two lightly buttered, ovenproof dishes and set aside. Plunge the plum tomatoes into boiling water, leave for a few seconds, then drain and peel off the skins. Cut in half lengthways and arrange around the kipper meat, rounded side uppermost. Using a small saucepan, warm the cream and whisk into it the mustard, curry powder and a pinch of salt, to taste. Pour this over the kipper and tomatoes and bake in the oven for 10–15 minutes, or until quietly bubbling and beginning to nicely gild all over. Some bread is essential here, I think.

lovely lamb

braised neck of lamb with carrots & pearl barley

serves 4

8 thick slices neck of lamb, approx. 1.2kg

salt and white pepper

2 large onions, halved and thinly sliced

7–8 smallish carrots, approx. 350g,
   peeled and quartered lengthways

400g smallish new potatoes, peeled

2 bay leaves

4–5 cloves

50g pearl barley

30g dripping or butter

1 heaped tbsp plain flour

a few shakes of Worcestershire sauce
   (optional)

2–3 tbsp chopped parsley

A favourite childhood recipe, this one, and equally divided between both Mum and Dad, as the cooks who made it. We probably ate it at least once a month during the colder months, maybe more. That familiar, most savoury and deep scent emanating from the bottom oven of the Aga when walking into the kitchen after a cold walk home from the school bus, was for this little boy, just the best smell in the whole world.

Occasionally – about twice a year, I reckon – Mum would mildly swear ('Blood and Sand!' was her favourite expletive), having forgotten to remove the freshly laundered washing from the drying rack, hauled up above said Aga, before she began to cook this marvellous braise. My brother and I thought this hilarious. Poor old Mum – and especially in the days before she had acquired a spin dryer …

And, by the way, she always added plenty of ready-ground white pepper (there was no other, then) to her lamb neck. I still so do, for that authentic memory, but you don't have to.

Note: if you wish to both be frugal and add extra flavour to the braise, then ladle off the surface fat (instead of using kitchen paper) from the settled lamb broth when it has finally emerged from the oven with the vegetables and meat together, and use some of it (instead of the dripping or butter) to make the roux with which to thicken the broth.

Preheat the oven to 170°C/325°F/gas mark 3.

Season the neck of lamb well, particularly with pepper, and put into a shallow, lidded casserole (one that will transfer from stove-top to oven), so that the slices sit tightly, almost as one layer. Pour over approx. 750ml of water, or to cover by about 1cm. Slowly bring up to a simmer, and skim off any scum that forms on the surface; I find that a few sheets of kitchen paper laid over the surface does the trick. Cover the pot and slide into the oven. Cook for 1 hour.

Remove the casserole, lift out the lamb and put on to a large plate, for the time being. Add the vegetables to the pot, stir them around and, over a low heat, once more bring the (now) lamb broth and vegetables back to a simmer. Remove any scum, as before. Reintroduce the lamb pieces to the pot, tucking them in and around the vegetables. Add the bay leaves, cloves and also the pearl barley, sprinkling it in here and there. Cover and return to the oven for a further hour, turning the temperature down a little if the liquid within is bubbling too fast – have a peek, occasionally.

Remove the pot and check to see if the lamb is tender – it should feel very tender when poked with a skewer – and that the vegetables, too, are well cooked through. If not, return to the oven for a further 20 minutes, or so. Now, lift out all the meat and vegetables from the pot and lay out on a large plate once more. Allow the broth to settle, then, once again (the last time, I promise), lift off any surface fat with more sheets of kitchen paper.

Melt the dripping or butter (unless you are using the fat from the braise, see page 117) in a small pan and stir in the flour. Cook gently together, stirring well, for 5 minutes or so, until the mixture (a roux) is golden brown. Whisk in a ladle or two of the broth to this, until smooth, then return to the majority of broth in the pot, further whisking everything together until it is a smooth gravy. Add Worcestershire sauce, if using, to taste. Bring this to a simmer, carefully return the meat and vegetables to the pot, and reheat for at least 15 minutes. Check the seasoning before finally stirring in the parsley. Serve this complete meal piping hot.

breast of lamb baked with onions

....

serves 4

1kg boned, rolled and tied lamb breast

salt and freshly ground white pepper

a little dripping or oil

1kg onions, thinly sliced

2 bay leaves

1 tbsp vinegar

2–3 tbsp anchovy essence, or to taste

2 tbsp finely chopped parsley

....

The Rhône meets Ramsbottom! Well … that's how I like to see the connection between a dish that Elizabeth David wrote about in *An Omelette and a Glass of Wine*, possibly my most favourite of all her books. In one chapter she describes a dish of beef and onions, ever so slowly braised in the ovens of barges, cooked by sailors on board, as these huge vessels chugged up and down the Rhône river. It brings to mind a romantic vision of an older France, together with the simple fact that strong, hard-working men need sustenance, but that it should be truly delicious sustenance and easy to cook in cramped, overheated conditions.

The basic premise is this: sliced beef, huge amounts of onions and no liquid. Cook for hours until done. In other words, great trays of this assembly are pushed into huge ovens and forgotten about. However, a magical thing happens when onions and meat are put together with added heat; they simply make their own gravy.

Once the beef is soft and tender, together with onions all slippery and golden, other flavours of the region are put into play, making the dish a work of genius. Chopped garlic and parsley (called 'persillade' in the Midi), vinegar for piquancy, some chopped anchovy for salt and finally, of course, local fruity olive oil for essential lubrication. Just perfect for the sunny Rhône valley, but maybe not for rainy old Ramsbottom, the Lancashire mill town very near to where I grew up.

That which I wanted to achieve was to turn the dish into a simple, inexpensive and homespun meal using breast of lamb. The particular ingredient used to season the barge beef, anchovies, brought to mind a wonderful bottle of pale brown British condiment, 'anchovy essence'. I have always loved this. The brand Burgess used to be my favourite, but I can't find it any more. So Geo Watkins it must be, for me; not as pink as Burgess, but it does the job. I felt that the garlic needed to go (you may disagree, and that's fine), but bay leaves I have added. No olive oil either, just a little natural, seeping fat from the lamb (the beef for the sailors was lean, so needed the oil). The inclusion of vinegar is unchanged, except that I am tempted to suggest a good shake of Sarson's, rather than 'un gout de vinaigre du vin', but that is entirely a matter for you, too. However, and finally, the parsley is unanimously essential to both.

Note: if you would like to prepare the leftover dish that follows from the lamb braise, make sure you cook extra meat or feed fewer.

Preheat the oven to 170°C/325°F/gas mark 3.

Season the lamb well on all surfaces. Melt the dripping/oil in a large, roomy, lidded pot until hot. Lay in the lamb breast, turn down the heat a little and colour well on all sides, until golden brown. Lift out the meat and remove all fat from the pot with a spoon. Tip in half the onions, then return the lamb to the pot and push it down into them. Pop in the bay leaves and cover with the rest of the onions.

Now, take a sheet of greaseproof paper and cut it into a circle slightly bigger than the diameter of the pot lid. Dampen it, lightly grease one side, and lightly press it over the onions (greased side down), while also against the side of the pot. This effects a kind of baffle over the lamb and onions, so that steam and juices stay intact, producing a moist and more flavoursome result (in professional kitchens, this paper covering is known as a 'cartouche'). Put on the lid, slide the pot into the oven and leave there for 1 hour.

Have a peek in the pot, now, and see how the onions are doing; they should be starting to collapse. Don't disturb them too much, but maybe scrape some down the side of the pot where they may have stuck a bit. You should, however, be able to see some of the natural juices of the onions seeping out and moistening the assembly. Replace the paper and lid, return the pot to the oven and continue to cook for a further hour. Note: if there are plenty of juices already visible at this stage, turn the oven down to 150°C/300°F/gas mark 2.

After 2 hours' cooking, the onions should now almost be swimming in juices. Push a skewer into the lamb to see how tender it is; there should be little resistance. Lift out the meat, put it into a small roasting tin and cover with foil. Turn down the oven again to 140°C/275°F/gas mark 1, and return the meat to the oven while you deal with the onions.

Remove the bay leaves. You will notice that a fair amount of fat has accumulated on the surface (lamb breast is a naturally fatty cut), so remove almost all of this with a few sheets of kitchen paper. Now, stir in the vinegar and anchovy essence, place the pot over a high heat and bring the onions and their juices to a simmer. Quietly reduce this mixture, stirring occasionally until sticky and beginning to become a deliciously unctuous mass; if you have ever made French onion soup, think of the early process of making that.

To finish the dish, check for seasoning; you should not need any extra salt, due to the anchovy essence, but I would always add more pepper at this stage as I like the dish quite so. Finally, stir in the parsley. Remove the lamb from the oven (if any meaty juices have exuded from the resting lamb, add them to the onions), cut off the strings and thickly slice the meat. Arrange the slices on a hot serving dish and pile the onions alongside. Mashed potatoes, anyone?

leftover cold breast of lamb, sliced, then breadcrumbed & fried till crisp, with garlic mayonnaise

serves 2

flour

beaten egg

dry breadcrumbs

dripping or oil, for frying

4 slices of cold, leftover cooked
   lamb breast (see previous recipe)

salt and freshly ground white pepper

for the garlic mayonnaise

2 egg yolks

2 cloves of garlic, crushed to a paste
   with a little sea salt

freshly ground white pepper

300–350ml olive oil, not too strong
   in flavour, but of good quality
   (if you find just olive oil too overpowering,
   use half olive oil and half sunflower
   oil, say)

lemon juice, to taste

Although I have removed the garlic from the braise in the previous dish, I feel moved to put it back into this very nice leftover. There is something so delicious about partnering meat that is crusted on the outside, while soft, a little fatty and moist on the inside, with a rich, emulsified and oily sauce. I'm telling you, it works really, really well.

Note: if you wish, use an electric hand-whisk for ease when making the mayonnaise.

First, to make the garlic mayonnaise, place the egg yolks in a bowl with the garlic and pepper. Beginning slowly, beat together while very, very slowly trickling in the olive oil. Once the mixture is becoming very thick, add a little lemon juice. Continue beating, adding the oil a little faster and speeding up the beating speed.

Taste the mayonnaise as you continue beating, and add a touch more lemon juice and more seasoning as you think necessary. Once you are happy with the flavour and texture – which should be almost ointment-like – the garlic mayonnaise is ready. Put to one side while you cook the lamb.

Have ready 3 shallow bowls filled with the following: flour, beaten egg and dry breadcrumbs. Take a solid frying pan (non-stick, if you prefer) and in it melt a tablespoon or so of the chosen fat – you may need more – then heat it to medium-hot. First, lightly season the lamb, then dust each slice with flour, then dip it into beaten egg and, finally, coat in the breadcrumbs. Shake off any excess and slide into the frying pan. Keeping the heat moderate, but quietly sizzling, allow one side to become a pale, golden brown before carefully turning over and doing the same to the other side. Lift out on to kitchen paper, place the slices on warmed plates and serve the garlic mayonnaise in a bowl on the side. Some cool and sprightly watercress would be good here.

grilled lamb cutlets with minted hollandaise

serves 2

1 rack of lamb, French-trimmed; that is,
  bones scraped clean and excess
  fat removed
salt and pepper
a little oil

for the minted hollandaise

3 tbsp white wine vinegar
3 tbsp water
1 small shallot, finely chopped
leaves from a small bunch of mint
3 egg yolks
200g unsalted butter, melted
salt and freshly ground white pepper
a touch of lemon juice

I first made this lovely sauce when working in west Wales in the early 1970s. We had been making its cousin, béarnaise sauce, for as long as we could remember and wanted to ring the changes. After much exhaustive book reading, we finally came across something known as 'sauce paloise'. Heaven knows its origins, or in which cookery book we found it, but it seemed a must to serve with the delicious local Welsh lamb from the butcher in St David's.

I have chosen to simply call it 'minted hollandaise', rather than 'sauce paloise' (or 'mint béarnaise', because of the essential tarragon in that sauce), mainly because it won't mean anything to anyone; well, maybe to a few dedicated sauce aficionados, but not in the general lexicon of culinary lotions.

Note: if you wish to use the traditional method for making hollandaise sauce, see the recipe for Smoked Haddock and Spinach with Chive Butter Sauce (page 107).

First make the sauce. Put the vinegar, water, the shallot and two-thirds of the mint leaves, chopped, into a small, stainless steel pan. Reduce over a moderate heat until syrupy. Strain this mixture through a fine sieve into the bowl of a small food processor. Add the egg yolks, switch on and process until airy and pale. Heat the butter until quite hot and bubbling (use a small pan with a lip, to aid pouring), then, with the motor running, slowly pour in the butter until the sauce has become thick, as with making mayonnaise; you may like to add a touch of the milky residue underneath the clear butter, as this processor method usually makes a thicker than usual sauce. Season lightly and add the remaining mint leaves. Briefly process once more, until the machine has chopped the leaves finely into the sauce. Squeeze in a touch of lemon juice, to taste. Pour into a sauceboat and keep warm.

Cut the rack of lamb into 6 cutlets, if small, and usually 8, if large. Lightly season them and brush with oil. Using a ribbed, stove-top grill (or a heavy, solid-based frying pan) on a high heat, grill the cutlets on each side for 2–3 minutes (medium-rare), 3–4 minutes (medium), and for about 5 minutes if you wish them to be medium-well to well done. Leave to rest for a few minutes before serving with the sauce. And chips – whichever way you like to make them – would be the perfect accompaniment.

marinated butterflied leg of lamb with Asian green sauce

serves 6–8

1 leg of lamb, butterflied, to give a rough
    boned weight of about 2–2.3kg
salt
oil

1 tsp ground cumin
1 tsp ground turmeric
½ tsp cayenne pepper
½ tsp paprika

for the marinade

150ml light soy sauce
50ml sesame oil
2 cloves of garlic, peeled and crushed
½ onion, peeled and chopped
big knob of fresh ginger, peeled and sliced
juice of 1 orange
juice of 1 lemon
1 tbsp muscovado sugar
1 dsp ground coriander

for the sauce

90g coriander leaves
40g mint leaves
8 cloves of garlic, peeled and crushed
2 tsp ground cumin
1 tsp sugar
1 heaped tsp sea salt
75ml lime juice
7–10 green chillies
200g Greek yoghurt

Lamb cooked in this way is terrifically tasty – whether marinated or not.
The skin of the meat sizzles and blisters almost to a blackened crust, in the
most agreeable fashion. I have cooked this on an open fire in Greece, where the
charcoal gives an incomparable flavour to the meat, but a ribbed stove-top grill
offers excellent results, too. Do make sure that you allow the lamb to rest once
cooked, as this will ensure an even pink – if you like it pink, that is – hue right
through the meat, while also keeping the juices intact when carving.

This is also particularly nice eaten with tzatziki (see page 38) on future
occasions, when you may enjoy a change from the green sauce, delicious as it is.
However, I am unsure as to whether one should serve both together, as there
may be a clash of culinary continents, here.

Liquidise all the ingredients for the marinade until as smooth as possible (pass through a sieve to be on the safe side, if you like). Lay the lamb in a large lidded pot or plastic box, and pour over the marinade. Massage the mixture into the meat, turning it over and over, until well coated. Cover with the lid (or clingfilm or kitchen foil) and put into the fridge for 24 – and up to 48 – hours, turning occasionally. Lift out the meat from the marinade, shake off excess liquid and drain well in a colander, say, then pat dry with kitchen paper. Season well with salt and smear oil over the entire surface; hands are best here.

Heat a large, stove-top ribbed grill to medium-hot or, even better, a charcoal-fired barbecue; this will give the most perfect and authentic results. Otherwise, preheat the oven to 200°C/400°F/gas mark 6, and put the lamb on a wire rack fitted inside a roasting dish.

If using the grill or barbecue method (the cook should keep the grill/coals at moderate to high temperature), lay the meat down and leave to quietly crust over the heat for about 20 minutes. Turn over and repeat (this is timed for nicely pink meat). If you choose to take the oven route, the turnings and timings remain about the same, but check that the lamb does not brown too much. Remove to a large serving platter and leave to rest for at least 10 minutes – and up to half an hour – while kept warm, loosely covered with foil if necessary (see page 320). Note: it is intentional that the surface will have become slightly blackened in parts, but the resultant pink inside contrasts winningly with the carbonised exterior.

Meanwhile, place all the green sauce ingredients in a small food processor and make a smooth, slack purée. Pour out into a bowl and set aside until the lamb is ready.

Transfer the lamb to a board and neatly carve into 0.5cm slices. Return them to the platter, collect any resultant juices and spoon over the meat. Serve with the green sauce and a plain green salad of, say, crisp Cos leaves simply dressed with lemon and olive oil.

nice rice

PRINCIPATO DI LUCEDIO

RISO SUPERFINO CARNAROLI

RISO NATURALE

rice with mussels & saffron

serves 2, generously, as a main dish,
   or 4 as a first course

2kg mussels, de-bearded and well washed

250ml dry sherry

2–3 tbsp olive oil

2 cloves of garlic, crushed and
   finely chopped

1 tsp curry powder

60g piquillo peppers, from a jar
   (the El Navarrico brand is excellent),
   finely chopped

pinch of dried chilli flakes

1 large tomato, peeled and chopped
   to a mush

250g carnaroli rice

1 tsp saffron threads

2 small spring onions, trimmed
   and finely chopped

1 tbsp chopped parsley

25g butter

I was unsure whether to refer to this as a pilaf, a kind of baked risotto sort of thing, or almost a faux Spanish paella. Prosaically, I finally decided upon the simple description of 'rice with mussels and saffron', for that is exactly what it is. And a very moreish result, be assured.

I use the Italian risotto rice, carnaroli. More than anything else, this particular rice is one of the easier ones to cook. In Venice, most cooks would probably use vialone nano, a smaller, tighter grain and, in fact, the most regularly employed when making seafood risotti in that city. Feel free to use it if you like. There is also absolutely no reason at all why one shouldn't use basmati rice (Tilda, for preference, as it always remains as nicely separate grains and rarely overcooks), turning this dish into a true seafood pilaf. Finally, the Spanish rice calasparra, the one for making paella, could further be an option. The choice is yours.

Preheat the oven to 190°C/375°F/gas mark 5.

First, check for any open mussels that refuse to close up again when briskly tapped; if they refuse to shut, discard them. Put the mussels into a large pot, pour over the sherry, bring up to a boil, then clamp on a lid and allow the mussels to cook for about a minute. Lift off the lid and shake the mussels about so that those underneath end up on top. Cook once more, lidded, for about the same time. Turn off the heat and check that the mussels have popped open; if not, cook for a touch longer. Drain through a colander suspended over another pan, shake them a little to dispel any liquid caught in the shells, and leave to drain for few minutes.

Shell the mussels (ditch any that stubbornly will not open), put the meat into a bowl and throw out the shells. Pour the mussel juice through a very fine sieve (to collect any grit or bits of shell) into a measuring jug. Top up with water to give a final measurement of 400ml. Using a solid, lidded pot, heat the olive oil and in it quietly fry the garlic, curry powder, peppers, chilli and tomato, until any liquid (from the tomato) has been driven off, and the mixture is almost a purée. Now add the rice and stir it around briskly, making sure that it is well coated and glistened by the oily mixture; add a touch more oil if you like. Pour in the liquid from the jug, add the saffron and bring the mixture to a simmer. Tip in the shelled mussels and stir well. Put on a lid and slide the pot into the oven. Cook for 20 minutes.

Remove the pot and leave to stand for 5 minutes without removing the lid. Take it off now, deftly stir in the spring onions, parsley and butter, place a tea-towel over the pot and clamp on the lid once more. Leave for a further 5 minutes, so allowing any excess steam to be absorbed and, also, to give a final swell to the rice; the final texture should be somewhere between a pilaf and a risotto. Serve directly from the pot, spooned on to hot plates. I see this gorgeous plate of food as a meal in itself, with no other accompaniment necessary.

buttered rice with mozzarella, garlic & basil

serves 2, generously

250g carnaroli rice

salt

200g buffalo mozzarella, cut into
    small chunks

100g freshly grated Parmesan,
    plus 2–3 tbsp extra

1 very small clove of garlic, crushed
    and finely chopped

bunch of basil, leaves only, roughly torn

50g softened, unsalted butter

freshly ground black pepper

This dish of rice emerges as a kind of boiled and sticky, nicely bland mock risotto. But, of course, it is no such thing; the process itself is against it from the start. Although the description 'boiled and sticky' may not exactly thrill the expectant taste buds, the assembly is a happy one – and it is very easy to prepare, too. Just think cooked rice and cheese, together with one of the most fragrant of all summer herbs, and with that lovely taste of creamy butter, too.

Boil the rice in about 1 litre of salted water, till just cooked. Briefly drain over a serving bowl, tip out the water (this has now heated the bowl), and now tip back half the drained rice into the hot bowl. Add the mozzarella, Parmesan, garlic, basil, butter and pepper, then cover with the rest of the rice and leave to settle for a minute or two. Now, stir vigorously, while also lifting and dropping back the rice, until the mozzarella becomes stringy – two large forks work best, here. Serve immediately on hot plates, and hand extra Parmesan at table.

risi e bisi

serves 4, as a first course

1kg fresh peas (unpodded weight), podded, and with the pods reserved

approx. 1 litre light chicken stock

75g butter

1 onion, very finely chopped

200g carnaroli rice

salt and freshly ground white pepper

3–4 tbsp freshly grated Parmesan

1 tbsp finely chopped parsley or, more controversially, mint

Again, to the Veneto, for one of the simplest and most perfect bowls of comfort eating: 'risi e bisi' – sloppy rice and peas. It is similar to a risotto with peas, but much more soupy in texture. I recall a very late springtime lunch enjoyed at Harry's Bar in Venice, fresh off the train from Florence, and at exactly the time when the first fresh peas had just come into season; but then, at Harry's, it would be unthinkable to serve this dish at any other time of year.

The risi e bisi was served in a deep bowl, filled to the brim, of the palest green and piping hot. Extra Parmesan was stirred in at table and that was my lunch. Just that. Well ... maybe a glass or two of prosecco, just to show willing.

By the way, do not worry that the peas will have lost a little of their bright colour by a more lengthy cooking than usual; peas do this naturally, but they also taste very good. I would say flavour over the look every time, with a dish such as this.

Note: although not exactly authentic, I sometimes like to use mint instead of parsley, here. Mainly, this is because I really like the taste of peas and mint together, which is a very English marriage. No doubt this would be deeply frowned upon by a strict Venetian cook, so I would change the name to 'sloppy rice and peas with mint'. That should do it.

Take the empty pea pods and place them in a food processor. Whiz to a coarse mush and put them into a large pan. Pour on the stock and simmer the mixture for about 30 minutes, until the stock is nicely pea-flavoured and lightly sweetened as a result. Strain through a fine sieve into a bowl and reserve.

Now, rinse out the pea-pod pan and in it melt 40g of the butter. Tip in the onion and fry over a medium heat until softened. Add the podded peas and gently cook for a minute or two, stirring frequently. Add 700ml of the pea-flavoured stock, cover, and cook at a moderate boil for 5 minutes.

Add the rice and the remaining pea stock, cover, and cook at a very slow simmer for 15–20 minutes, or until the rice is tender but just firm to the bite. Stir occasionally while cooking; also taste and add a touch of seasoning (don't forget that salty Parmesan will be added later). Just prior to serving, briskly stir in the remaining butter, 2 tablespoons of Parmesan and the parsley or mint. Pour into hot bowls and offer extra cheese at table.

chicken
with livers

chicken

poached chicken with saffron sauce & cucumber

....

serves 2

for the chicken

1 x 1.5kg chicken, preferably corn-fed

1 onion, stuck with 3 cloves

2 sticks of celery, chopped

1 carrot, thickly sliced

1 leek, cleaned, trimmed and thickly sliced

2 large tomatoes, roughly chopped

2 bay leaves

2–3 sprigs of thyme

small bunch of parsley, roughly chopped

250ml dry white wine

salt

for cooking the cucumbers and making the sauce

300ml of the chicken broth

4–6 small cucumbers, depending on size, or 1 medium-sized normal cucumber, halved, then each half cut into quarters lengthways

1 dsp pastis, optional, but essential, for me

25g butter

1 rounded dsp flour

1 tsp saffron threads

100ml double cream

salt and freshly ground white pepper

small squeeze of lemon juice (optional)

....

Here is a very nice way to enjoy two meals from one small chicken. The first recipe uses only the breasts of the bird, but taken from a chicken cooked whole, with vegetables and aromatics, making a lovely broth as a matter of course. The second, a perky salad using the thigh and drumstick joints, is something to have the following day, or even the day after that. If there is some broth left, keep the joints covered in that, carefully stored in the fridge.

This breast dish is a relatively posh one, with quite a rich sauce and some delicious hot cucumbers as an accompanying vegetable. It is not often one eats cooked cucumber but, believe me, it is unusually delicate and a fine partner to the saffron flavour. I have a Lebanese grocer's quite near to where I live, so quite regularly I acquire some small cucumbers from them – the only ones they actually stock, in fact. These suit this dish both for a particularly fragrant flavour, and for their diminutive shape, so nice when left entire.

The second outing, the salad (page 149), is a simple assembly of crunchy-crisp skin, moist chicken (the original poaching helps, here), salad greens, cucumber – again, but more usually, raw – and a rather jolly, sweet mustard dressing. The contrast between hot chicken, cool salady things and this kind of sweet-sour lubrication is a winning one. I only hope that you will think so, too.

Put the chicken into a roomy pot, breast side up, and make sure there is enough room around the bird to also accommodate the flavouring vegetables and herbs. Add these, then pour in the wine and sprinkle over a little salt. Pour in enough water so that it does not entirely cover the chicken; try to leave the breasts about a quarter exposed, because the leg and thigh joints (immersed in the liquid) take much longer to cook than the breasts which will, effectively, steam.

Place over a moderate heat and allow to come up to a simmer. When a fair amount of unsightly grey scum has accumulated on the surface, start to skim this off with a large spoon until almost none remains; a little more will be generated throughout the cooking time, but remove that when and if necessary. Now let the chicken cook very gently for 45–50 minutes, covered. Keep a keen eye on the proceedings, as you only want the broth to gently blip, not boil. After the time has elapsed, switch off the heat and leave to rest in the broth, still covered, for a further 15 minutes.

Lift out the bird, flick off any bits of stray vegetable matter and place on a dish. Strain the broth into a bowl using a fine sieve and discard the exhausted vegetables. Wipe out the original cooking pot and return the chicken to it. Return the cooking broth to the chicken in its pot and keep warm, covered.

To cook the cucumbers, first measure off about 300ml of the broth surrounding the chicken. Put the cucumbers into a medium-sized saucepan that will accommodate them snugly. Pour over the broth, add the pastis (if using) and simmer the cucumbers until tender when poked with a skewer; they should be soft, but not on the verge of collapse. Remove them with a slotted spoon and put to keep warm with the remaining broth surrounding the chicken. Keep the cucumber cooking liquid to hand.

To make the saffron sauce, melt the butter in another small pan and stir in the flour to make a roux. Cook for a minute or two, then start to whisk in the cucumber cooking liquid until smooth and beginning to thicken. Allow to simmer very gently, stirring regularly, for about 10 minutes, before sprinkling in the saffron. Stir it in (don't use a whisk, as all the saffron stamens will become entangled in it), switch off the heat and cover the pan, so allowing the saffron to infuse in the sauce, for about 5 minutes. Now add the cream, a little salt and pepper, and allow to come back to a simmer. Add a squeeze of lemon juice, for a sharper edge to the sauce.

To serve, take the chicken from the pot and carve off the breasts. Remove the skin from each breast and cut the chicken in slanting slices. Lay on 2 hot plates, arrange the cucumbers alongside and spoon over plenty of the saffron sauce. Some small, peeled new potatoes would be very nice here, too, if you wished.

hot chicken salad with sweet mustard dressing

serves 2, generously

salt and freshly ground white pepper

2 cooked chicken legs

a little sunflower oil

2 big handfuls of salad greens: mâche
    (lamb's lettuce), watercress, rocket
    (if you must), small spinach leaves
    or a mixture of all four

a tiny squeeze of lemon juice

a little olive oil

a little finely chopped shallot
    (or chives or spring onion)

some peeled and sliced cucumber

for the dressing

1–2 tbsp smooth Dijon mustard

1 rounded tsp caster sugar or, if you happen
    to have some, 2 tsp syrup from a jar of
    preserved ginger

salt and freshly ground white pepper

a squeeze of lemon juice, to taste

a few drops of Tabasco sauce

4–5 tbsp sunflower oil

2–3 tbsp hot – but not boiling – water

Using a small food processor, ideally, blend together the first 5 dressing ingredients until smooth. With the motor running, gradually add the oil and water, alternately, until an homogenous dressing is realised. Pour into a small bowl and set aside.

Season the chicken legs and very quietly fry them, skin side down in the sunflower oil, in a frying pan until the skin is really crisp; anything up to a slow 10–15 minutes, and do not rush them. Turn over and do the other side, but for not as long a time – it is the skin that you need to be crisp, for a sensational hot salad. Cut the chicken meat away from the bones and roughly slice. Keep hot.

To serve, put the salad greens into a bowl, season them, then briefly dress with lemon juice and oil. Pile on to 2 plates, sprinkle with the shallot and surround with cucumber slices. Pile the chicken on top of the greens and, without drowning the salad, spoon over some of the dressing. Eat forthwith, while the chicken remains crisp and hot.

homemade tandoori chicken

serves 4

approx. 1.5–1.75kg chicken drumsticks, skinned

juice of 2 small lemons, plus extra lemons to squeeze over once the chicken is cooked

salt

500g plain and runny yoghurt (absolutely not thick Greek)

3–4 tbsp tandoori spice mix (a good brand, preferably from an Asian shop)

I know that it is incredibly easy, almost everywhere, to phone up a local Indian restaurant or takeaway and have endless boxes of tandoori chicken delivered to the door, day in, day out. And, what's more, it will, almost without exception, have been cooked in a traditional and authentic tandoor oven, to boot. So, why make your own, I hear you ask?

Well, I just love making it, that's all. And, it is hot and juicy, directly from my hot oven and grill. And, it is not lukewarm and dried out a bit, as some delivered versions can often be. And, if you are having it in warm weather and own a barbecue, then the charcoal flavour given to the drumsticks as they grill can, really quite nicely, offer that scorched and smoky flavour redolent of the big clay oven in the kitchens of your local Gujerati Garden or Bombay Palace. If I could also give you a decent recipe for naan bread, I would, but my feeble attempts at making that particular dough have usually ended up in the bin. Breadmaking has never been my forte. One should be utterly useless at a few things, don't you think?

Using a small, sharp knife, cut deep slashes into the chicken flesh without going right down to the bone. Put into a bowl and sprinkle with the lemon juice and salt, massaging these into the chicken until well mixed. Leave to macerate for about an hour. Whisk together the yoghurt and tandoori spice in a bowl and pour over the chicken. Again, mix well until the entire bowlful is a wonderful red. Cover with clingfilm and put into the fridge for at least 5–6 hours, or overnight, occasionally turning the chicken around a bit.

Preheat the oven to 230°C/450°C/gas mark 8.

Lift out the drumsticks from the tandoori mixture and gently shake off any excess. Place a wire rack over a roasting tin and lay the chicken legs upon it (it is a good idea, washing-up wise, to line the tin with foil, as the drippings from the chicken will burn). Bake in the oven for about 20 minutes, or until the drumsticks are richly burnished and almost blackened in parts; if not, finish them under a hot grill.

Eat using your fingers, and squeeze more lemon over them as you go. And, if you would like a simple dip of some sort, add some freshly chopped mint and a chopped green chilli to some seasoned yoghurt.

chicken livers

chicken livers &
mushrooms on toast

....

serves 2

50g butter

salt and freshly ground black pepper

200g trimmed chicken livers

1 shallot, finely chopped

1 clove of garlic, finely chopped

100g open-cup mushrooms, thickly sliced

4 tbsp Madeira

100ml double cream

1 tsp very finely chopped rosemary leaves

2 large, thick slices of white bread, toasted

....

For me, the archetypal kind of Sunday supper dish – which should always involve toast, somewhere. Whether it be simple scrambled or poached eggs, anchovies or thin slices of Parma ham, even baked beans, for heaven's sake, hot buttered toast must feature. This chicken liver/mushroom thing, however, is a notch above the norm and is originally based upon my Dad's mushrooms on toast; a regular, family supper of which we never tired. Funny thing was, however, they always turned out as near as dammit to a heated-up can of Chesswood creamed mushrooms. But, as I always watched him make them, I knew different. He was a master of the mushroom, Dad, when creaming away at the Aga.

Melt the butter in a frying pan until foaming. Season the livers and briefly fry in the butter until golden brown; they should be slightly bouncy to the touch and very pink in the middle (they will be further cooked, later). Transfer the livers to a plate and keep warm.

In the butter left in the pan, fry the shallot and garlic until golden. Add the mushrooms and quietly cook for a further 2–3 minutes; add a touch more butter if necessary. Add the Madeira to the pan and reduce until syrupy, then pour in the cream and add the rosemary. Bring to a simmer and allow the cream to thicken to a rich sauce before returning the livers to the pan. Check for seasoning, heat the livers through and spoon over hot toast – buttered or not, but the dish is quite rich anyway.

chicken liver mousse
with port jelly

makes 4 small ramekins

125g chicken (or duck) livers,
   trimmed of any blemishes
2 egg yolks
50g unsalted butter, softened
50g duck/goose fat, softened
   (but not liquid)
½ tsp salt

4–5 grindings of black pepper
a little freshly grated nutmeg
pinch of sugar
1 tbsp Cognac or Armagnac
125ml double cream
a little extra butter, melted

Some may wish to say that this dish is similar to the now ubiquitous chicken liver parfait offered on the menu of almost every single 'fine dining' (always pronounced 'fane daning', by me) restaurant. Well, as quite often foie gras is included in the make-up of most of those parfaits, that observation would fall to the ground to start with. The description of very, very smooth, however, is common to both preparations; silky smooth, even, and pale pink within.

Now then, when I feel in the mood, I make a port jelly to pour on top of these delectable mousses. The following recipe simply advises some melted butter to seal the surface of the mousse, once cooked and cooled. But if you want to have a go at this jelly, then I shall run through the ingredients and method now ...

You will need about 500ml of well-seasoned, cold chicken stock; 3 egg whites; about 200g of minced turkey; 3 leaves of gelatine and 75ml of port. Put the stock into a roomy pan and mix together the egg whites and turkey until well blended. Tip this into the stock and briefly whisk together. Change to a wooden spoon (the whisk eventually becomes clogged with turkey bits, otherwise) and place the pan over a moderate heat. Begin to stir the mixture while it heats up, and just before it approaches a gentle simmer, turn the heat down to very low. Leave to cook, just at an occasional blip, for about 45 minutes. By now, the liquid beneath the turkey mince – a rather

unappetising, grey mulch – should be crystal clear. Put the gelatine leaves into a bowl and pour over some cold water.

Lay a scrupulously clean tea-towel (or a sheet of double-folded muslin) inside a colander and place over a bowl. Now, carefully make a hole in the turkey mulch with a spoon, then ladle out the clear stock and pour it into the towel-lined colander, so that any bits will be caught. Once this is finished, lift out the colander and discard the exhausted turkey mulch.

Lift out the gelatine leaves from their cold water, squeeze out any excess water, and add to the hot stock, where they will melt. Stir in the port and leave the stock to become cool, but still liquid. At the end of the mousse recipe below, where instructed to pour melted butter over the top, simply replace the butter with some of this delicious jelly, which will then set upon the surface, once chilled in the fridge for a few hours.

Note: please watch out for lingering washing powder odours if using a tea-towel to strain the stock, as these can taint the jelly. And how horrible that would be!

Preheat the oven to 150°C/300°F/gas mark 2, and also boil a kettle.

Using a food processor or liquidiser, blend the livers, egg yolks, butter, fat, seasonings, sugar and alcohol until very smooth. Heat the cream in a small, preferably lipped pan, until hot, not boiling. With the processor/liquidiser motor running on low, pour in the hot cream until well blended. Check for salt.

Pour the mixture through a fine sieve into a bowl, then ladle it into 4 ramekins until almost full. Place the mousses in a deep roasting tin and pour water from the boiled kettle around the ramekins until almost matching the level of the interior filling. Cover the ramekins with a single, flat sheet of foil, but don't tighten it around the tin.

Bake the mousses in the oven for about 20 minutes, or until only just set (think caramel custard – just wobbling, if nudged), and check them frequently. Once cooked, remove from the water and leave to cool to room temperature. Spoon over a generous film of melted butter and place in the fridge to set. Best eaten after 24 hours, with very thin, hot toast.

a simple chicken liver & pork terrine, with green peppercorns

....

serves 8–10

500g chicken livers, trimmed,
   coarsely minced

300g skinless, fatty belly pork,
   coarsely minced

250g excellent-quality sausages,
   skins removed

4 cloves of garlic, crushed and chopped

2 tbsp chopped parsley

2 rounded tsp herbes de Provence

6 cloves, but only the tiny ball on the tip,
   pinched off and crumbled between
   the fingers

5–6 healthy rasps from a whole nutmeg

2 tsp sea salt

100ml Cognac

75ml Madeira or sherry
   (amontillado, say, but not dry)

1 tbsp green peppercorns,
   from a jar or tin, drained

....

First of all, it is essential to start preparing this lovely terrine the day before
you make it. You could leave the mixture to mature for a few hours, but a good
12 hours, at least, is most beneficial to the final taste.

   I have always enjoyed making terrines or pâtés in old-fashioned, foil
takeaway containers. They freeze well in these for one thing but, more
importantly, they make excellent gifts for friends; you don't need to ask for the
dish back or forget where it went in the first place ... I don't know anyone who
doesn't like to have homemade pâté in the fridge, to cut at occasionally, with
a thin slice of toast and an early evening glass of wine.

   Note: a home mincer is a most useful attachment to a domestic kitchen,
whether manual or electrically driven. How many butchers do you know who
will mince chicken livers for you, anyway? If taking the food processor route,
please make sure that the pulse button is employed using a tentative digit.

Mix everything together in a large bowl or, for ease, the bowl of an electric food mixer using the flat beater. Tip into a plastic box, say, put on a lid and keep in the fridge overnight.

The next day, first preheat the oven to 190°C/375°F/gas mark 5.

Pile the mixture into a terrine mould of about 1 litre capacity or, if you like, use 3 or 4 foil takeaway containers (see above). Smooth the surface using your hand, first dipped into warm water – this really helps – leaving a very slightly domed finish to the mixture. Place the terrine(s) into a deep roasting tin and surround with tap-hot water. Loosely drape a sheet of kitchen foil over the terrine(s), but don't tighten it around the tin. Cook in the oven for about 1½ hours if in one single container, or for slightly less – say 1 hour – if using foil containers.

Remove the sheet of foil for the last 10–15 minutes, so allowing the top of the terrine to brown a little. Once cooked, remove from the oven, take the terrine(s) out of the roasting tin and leave to cool completely at room temperature. Wrap the terrine(s) in clingfilm and put into the fridge. Ideally, leave there for 2 days – and up to 5 – before cutting into thick slices, directly from the container. Eat with hot, buttered toast and cornichons.

spiced chicken liver pilau

....

serves 4, for a light lunch, say

2 tbsp oil

400g fresh chicken livers, well trimmed
   and cut in half

50g butter

1 large onion, peeled and finely chopped

2 cloves of garlic, peeled and sliced

1 scant tbsp coriander seeds, crushed

5 cloves

4 cardamom pods, lightly crushed

2 large pinches of dried chilli flakes

300g basmati rice (Tilda brand, preferably)

450ml chicken stock

1 heaped tbsp currants

4–5 strips of lemon zest

salt and freshly ground black pepper

2 tbsp coarsely chopped coriander leaves

2 limes, halved

....

I cannot call this fragrant dish of rice anything other than a pilau, as it leans so much more towards the Asian than it does to the French pilaf, simply because of the spices involved. That being said, the process involving rice ratio to liquid remains, as always, the same: volume or weight of rice to one and a half of liquid. Veer not from this directive at your peril.

Note: many will say that rice needs to be washed, rinsed and soaked before beginning to make a pilaf/pilau. However, when using a very good-quality basmati rice (such as Tilda) I have never found this to be necessary. Moreover, when I have done this washing and soaking business in the past, occasionally thinking I should because my peers have talked of it so insistently, hey presto! – my pilaf has overcooked, perfectly.

Preheat the oven to 190°C/375°F/gas mark 5.

Heat the oil in a heavy-based, lidded pot until almost smoking. Add the chicken livers in a single layer and briefly fry on each side for seconds only; they must still be undercooked within. Lift out and put on to a plate. Add the butter to the pot, fry the onions and garlic until pale gold, then stir in the coriander, cloves, cardamom and chilli. Tip in the rice and gently stir around for a couple of minutes until it is well coated with butter. Pour in the stock and bring up to a simmer. Tip in the currants and lemon zest, taste the liquid and then season with salt and pepper. Bring up to a simmer and now reintroduce the chicken livers, burying them underneath the rice. Switch off the heat, put on the lid and cook in the oven for 20 minutes.

Remove from the oven, but don't take the lid off for a further 5 minutes; this allows the pilau to finish cooking. Gently fluff up the rice with 2 forks, taking care not to break up the livers, while also deftly mixing in the chopped coriander. Serve directly from the pot on to hot plates. Hand the limes separately, so that each person may spritz their own serving.

ham, bacon &
a little pig

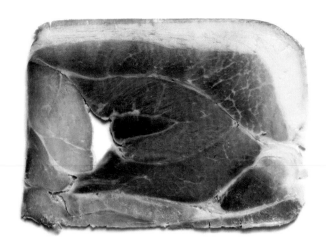

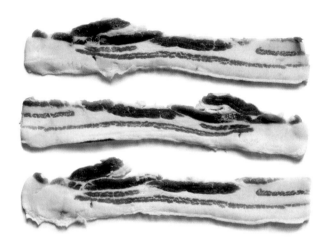

délices d'Argenteuil

....

serves 4

16 asparagus spears, trimmed and peeled

8 very thin slices Parma ham

for the pancake batter

100g flour

2 eggs

large pinch of salt

250ml milk

50g butter, melted, plus extra for cooking
the pancakes

for the hollandaise sauce

3 egg yolks

250g unsalted butter, melted

a little salt and freshly ground pepper

juice of ½ a lemon

....

These utterly delicious pancakes hark back to my initial apprenticeship during
the school holidays, aged sixteen, in a French restaurant called La Normandie,
a few miles away from where I grew up, in Bury, Greater Manchester (then
Lancashire). Although this is not their first outing from me, it is seventeen
years since I first referred to them in *Roast Chicken and Other Stories* (Ebury
Press, 1994), so do please make some if they are new to you or when you feel
in the mood to make pancakes, together with the accompanying hollandaise
sauce. Also, try to wait for an English spring, when our home-grown asparagus
is in season.

To make the pancake batter, whisk the flour, eggs, salt and half the milk together
in a mixing bowl until smooth. Add the butter and enough of the remaining milk to
achieve a thin, pouring cream consistency. Leave to stand for 30 minutes. To make the
pancakes, use a 20cm, preferably non-stick frying pan (or a favourite pancake pan if
you have a nicely 'seasoned' one) and in it melt a small amount of butter. Allow it to
become hot and sizzling, then pour in enough batter to thinly cover the base of the
pan. This first pancake is usually a bit of a mess, so chuck it out and start afresh.
Now, without greasing the pan again, make 8 thin pancakes and put to one side.

To make the hollandaise sauce, whisk together the egg yolks with a tiny splash of water in a stainless-steel pan over a very low heat, until thick and smooth. Now, off the heat, continue to whisk while pouring in the melted butter in a thin stream, leaving behind the milky residue that has settled in the bottom of the butter pan. Season the sauce and sharpen with lemon juice, to taste. Keep warm.

Preheat the oven to 180°C/350°F/gas mark 4, and a grill to hot.

Boil the asparagus in well-salted water for about 5 minutes or until tender when pierced with a sharp knife. Once done, lift them out with a slotted spoon and drain on a tea-towel.

To assemble the délices, take a pancake, lay upon it a slice of ham, then arrange 3 asparagus spears on top. Roll up and place in a lightly buttered baking dish. Bake in the oven for about 15–20 minutes, or until just beginning to crisp at the edges. To make absolutely sure that they are heated through, pierce one with a thin skewer, leave for 5 seconds and lightly press against your bottom lip. If only warm, give them a few more minutes.

Remove the délices to a warmed serving dish and coat each one carefully with a spoonful of hollandaise sauce, running it along their length. Very briefly flash the délices under the grill until only just gilded by the heat. Serve at once.

fried ham & cheese sandwich

....

serves 2

4 slices of thin, white bread
(square in shape)

4 thin slices of cooked ham

olive oil

for the sandwich filling

250g grated Gruyère

2 small egg yolks

1 tbsp Worcestershire sauce

1 rounded tsp mustard powder

2 pinches of cayenne pepper

a few shakes of Tabasco sauce
(optional, but it gives a nice extra kick)

a little salt

a touch of cream, but only if you think
the mixture too thick, once made

....

These incredibly moreish sandwiches are based upon those served at Harry's Bar, in Venice. If actually sitting at the bar at Harry's, they are casually offered to those sitting there, maybe, like me sipping an ice-cold Martini. It is impossible to refuse – although be aware that they may easily appear on your drinks bill ...

Very yummy chicken croquettes might also make occasional appearances, but it is this variation on the French 'croque monsieur' that wins hands down, every time. The original recipe comes from *The Harry's Bar Cookbook* (first published in Great Britain by Smith Gryphon, 1991).

Note: the filling quantity will give you far more than you need for the following recipe, but it keeps well in the fridge for a week. It further freezes well, packed into small, lidded pots for future occasions.

Put all the filling ingredients (except the cream) into the bowl of a food processor and blend until smooth; it should be easily spread, so now add the cream if needed. Spoon out into a plastic box, cover and keep in the fridge until ready to use.

Take a slice of bread, cover with a thin layer of cheese mixture almost to the edge, place a slice of ham over that and finally place another slice of bread on the ham.

Press down firmly and then repeat the process for the second sandwich. Cut off the crusts and liberally brush (or spray) each side of the sandwiches with olive oil.

Now, heat a large, non-stick frying pan until medium-hot. Cut each sandwich in half to give 4 rectangles, and fry in the dry pan until gorgeously golden and crusted on each side – about 2 minutes per side. Eat forthwith, and not without napkins.

quiche Lorraine

....

serves 4

for the pastry
60g butter
60g lard
200g plain flour
pinch of salt
2–3 tbsp ice-cold water

for the filling
10–12 thin rashers of smoked streaky
    bacon, cut into slivers
4 egg yolks
3 whole eggs
400ml whipping cream
a little salt and much freshly ground
    white pepper
a generous scraping from a whole nutmeg

....

Pedant that I am, it had always annoyed me that, when fashioning a lovely quiche Lorraine, the little chunks of bacon always sank to the bottom of the pastry case while the quiche cooked. As I have always preferred a deepish enclosure to the custard filling, this irritating scenario soon became tiresome, and needed solving. And why was it that the same quiche in a fine Parisian pâtisserie had nicely golden bits of bacon poking up out of its eggy surface, and mine did not? Well, the trick is to use the thinnest bacon slices rather than, say lardons (so readily available now, ready cut, I know) and cut them into small slivers. These will then float to the surface, but also nicely suspend themselves throughout the mixture as it sets.

Result, as they say.

To make the pastry, cut the butter and lard into small chunks and place in a large bowl with the flour and salt. Gently rub the fat into the flour using fingertips until the texture resembles very coarse breadcrumbs. Mix in only just enough water to bind the mixture together. Lightly knead this dough until well amalgamated, dust with flour and slip into a plastic bag. Place in the fridge for 30 minutes before using.

Preheat the oven to 180°C/350°F/gas mark 4 and also place a flat baking sheet in there, which will help to cook the base of the quiche more evenly.

Roll out the pastry as thinly as possible, use to line a 20cm wide by 4cm deep tart tin, lightly prick the base with a fork all over, then bake blind. This is done by lining the uncooked pastry case with a sheet of kitchen foil and filling with some dried haricot beans, for instance. It is then cooked for about 15–20 minutes on the flat baking sheet, removed from the oven, and the foil and beans transferred to a container for future use. Return the pastry case to the oven for a further 10 minutes or so, until it is pale golden, crisp and well cooked through, particularly the base.

Lightly fry the bacon in a dry, non-stick frying pan for a minute or two, until crisp and some of the fat has run out. Drain on kitchen paper and spread out evenly over the base of the cooked tart case. Whisk the egg yolks and whole eggs together, stir in the cream and season with salt, pepper and nutmeg. Pour the custard into the pastry case and cook for 30–40 minutes, or until nicely puffed and the surface of the custard is pale golden and just set. Eat warm, or at room temperature. Hot quiche, straight from the oven, does not taste good; it will, in fact, be taste-less.

braised pork shin with saffron mashed potatoes

....

serves 2

25g butter

2 tbsp olive oil

salt and freshly ground black pepper

4 chunky pieces of pork shin (osso buco),
  approx. 750–850g

a little flour

1 onion, finely chopped

at least ½ a bottle of drinkable,
  dry white wine

a touch of lemon juice

2–3 sprigs of sage

for the saffron mashed potatoes

750g floury potatoes, peeled and
  cut into chunks

1 tsp saffron threads

1 clove of garlic, peeled and crushed
  to a paste with a little salt

75ml milk

75–100ml extra virgin olive oil

for the gremolata

zest from ½ a small orange, in strips

a small handful of parsley sprigs

1 small clove of garlic, peeled and bruised

....

I am very pleased with the idea for this recipe, as it includes a favourite cut of meat married to a special dish of mine, that of mashed potatoes flavoured with saffron. For those who are familiar with the great Milanese dish of 'Osso buco alla Milanese' (slowly braised veal shin served with saffron risotto) – the answer lies there. So I was especially thrilled to find freshly prepared, chunky slices of pork shin in the butchery department of my local supermarket one day and the idea began to grow. Also, the notion of a gremolata with orange zest instead of the more familiar lemon is an unusually fragrant addition.

  The care involved in the cooking of this dish is, essentially, a labour of love. The following method is one of my most favourite of all Italian braises, and is based upon the preparation known as 'in bianco'. This is simply onions and white wine, with definitely no tomato. The meat is lightly floured, nicely coloured in a mixture of olive oil and butter, the excess fat tipped away and wine intermittently introduced over a slow and gentle heat, until the juices are syrupy and well flavoured.

Melt the butter and olive oil in a heavy-based deep pot – of a size that will hold the pieces of meat in a single layer – and heat the fats until they are beginning to froth. Season the pork pieces and dip lightly into the flour. Shake off any excess and put them into the pan. Fry on both sides, until each surface is crusted and golden brown. Remove the pork to a plate and tip out all but a spoonful of fat. Add the onion to the pot, quietly stew these until well coloured, then return the pork to the pot.

Reduce the heat and pour in a glass of wine. Allow to bubble up and turn down the heat even further. Partially cover the pan and simmer so gently that the liquid merely shudders from time to time. Turn the meat over once the wine has reduced somewhat and add a little more wine, along with the lemon juice and sage. Cover and braise for a further 30 minutes. Check occasionally that the wine has not evaporated too much. If so, again, add some more wine. The total cooking time should not be much longer than 1½ hours. Eventually, the winey gravy should only just be enough to sauce the meat; say a couple of tablespoons for each serving. Keep the pork warm, covered.

Meanwhile, boil the potatoes in lightly salted water until tender. Warm together the saffron, garlic, milk and olive oil in a small pan. Cover and infuse for 10 minutes. Drain the potatoes well; dry out in the oven if they seem excessively wet. Pass the potatoes through a mouli-légumes or potato ricer into a heated bowl, then add the saffron mixture in a thin stream, beating energetically with a wooden spoon; don't use a whisk, as the saffron stamens will become all entangled in it. When all the saffron infusion has been added, continue to beat and lighten it.

When ready to serve the dish, quickly make the gremolata. Simply put the orange strips, parsley and garlic together on a board and, using a sharp, heavy knife, chop them together until fine. Reheat the pork, fish out the sage and discard, then transfer 2 pieces of pork to 2 hot plates, together with their gravy. Spoon some of the saffron mashed potatoes alongside and, finally, sprinkle some of the gremolata over the meat. A complete dish, with deeply savoury qualities.

cotechino sausage, lentils & mustard fruits

....

serves 2, generously, as a main course

1 pre-cooked cotechino sausage
(see below), heated according
to instructions

for the lentils

3 tbsp olive oil

1 small onion, finely chopped

2 cloves of garlic, finely chopped

125g lentils, either Italian Castellucio
or French Puy

1 bay leaf

freshly ground black pepper

salt

a small slice of butter

2 tsp smooth Dijon mustard

a trickle of red wine vinegar

to serve

mustard fruits (mostarda di Cremona,
see below)

....

An Italian cotechino sausage, pre-prepared, foil-packed and cooked in its
own fat and juices, is a marvellous, almost instant meal – and taken directly
from the store cupboard whenever you fancy it; I, for one, am rarely without
a cotechino to hand.

They are readily available from good Italian delis, packed in handsome
boxes, and offer a generous shelf life. You should not, at all, ever feel guilty
about this most useful of 'ready meals'. They are incredibly tasty, highly
seasoned and with a rich flavour. If you have never eaten one, I urge you to
search them out.

Conveniently, similar provenders will also stock jars of sticky 'mostarda
di Cremona' (the northern Italian city where it originates). This sweet and
'hot' conserve consists of preserved fruits – cherries, peaches, melon rind,
pears, etc. – soaked in a sweet syrup infused with pungent mustard oil. Some
brands are hotter then others, but the most common I have seen in the UK is
Sperlari, available online.

However, the finest mostarda I have ever purchased was in the fabulous
food store Peck, in Milan. Stock up there if you ever visit that city.

Furthermore, if you want the treat of your life, gourmet-wise, Peck is the finest food emporium I know, anywhere.

Heat the olive oil in a stainless steel or other non-reactive saucepan and fry the onion and garlic until soft. Add the lentils and stir so that they are well coated and glisten. Cover with water by about 5cm, pop in the bay leaf and grind in plenty of pepper; do not add any salt now, as it has a tendency to harden the lentils while they cook (if you need any extra water, add it from a boiled kettle). Gently simmer the lentils, uncovered, for 30–40 minutes or so, until they are just cooked and most of the water has been absorbed. Remove the bay leaf and, only now, season with salt to taste. Stir in the butter, mustard and vinegar. Keep the lentils hot, covered.

Remove the cotechino from its cooking packet, stir any juices into the lentils, and serve them both piping hot, the sausage thickly sliced, and with some of the mustard fruits, roughly sliced, as a deliciously sweet and pungent condiment.

four small
birds,
a big duck,
a small bit
of rabbit

pot-roast quails with verjuice & grapes

....

serves 2

1 small lemon, cut into quarters

4 quails

salt and freshly ground white pepper

50g cold butter, diced

200ml verjuice

2–3 tbsp chicken stock

20 seedless grapes, peeled, if it pleases ...

....

Some folk don't get quails and I have never understood quite why. They taste very good indeed when carefully cooked. The finest ones that I have ever eaten (about twenty years ago, now) emerged from a revolving spit, within an enormous fireplace and cooked over an enormous log fire by our host Helen Hamlyn (widow of my partner at Bibendum, then, the late Paul Hamlyn), in their house in Gloucestershire. In fact, not only were they the best quails I have ever eaten, I am not so sure they were not one of the most delicious plates of food full stop. I guess, however, that they were made even more memorable by a lump of black truffle wrapped in a slice of fatty bacon, that had been pushed inside them while they cranked away, before being done to a turn, as they turned on the spit ...

Here, they are more prosaically pot-roasted with verjuice and grapes, but are none the worse for that; one would not wish to diminish my diminutive birds simply because they don't have a lovely truffle up their bottom. Verjuice is an acidic juice made from the pressing of unripe grapes, then bottled. The maker of this cooking condiment that has most pleased me in the past is one made by Australian Maggie Beer.

Note: if you can find them, large, well-fed French quails will appeal more than the smaller, less plump British birds.

Preheat the oven to 200°C/400°F/gas mark 6.

Squeeze a little lemon juice over the quails, then put a lemon quarter into the cavity of each one. Season with salt and pepper. Melt about 25g of the butter in a frying pan and brown the little birds gently on all sides until golden – about 5 minutes. Arrange them in a deep, lidded and heavy-based pot, pour in the verjuice and bake in the oven for 10 minutes, covered. Remove from the oven, turn the quails over, and cook for another 10 minutes. Turn off the oven, lift out the quails from the pot and keep warm in the waning heat of the oven, its door ajar.

Place the pot on a moderate heat, add the stock and grapes and cook until the sauce is reduced by half – or, at least, until beginning to turn a touch syrupy. Swirl in the remaining diced, cold butter to finish the sauce. Check for seasoning, pour the sauce over the quails and serve immediately, with creamed potatoes, I think.

Note: if you like, extract the lemon quarters from inside the quails and squash them into the sauce as you eat, for a sharper finish to the dish.

pigeon & mushroom pie

serves 4

25g butter

175g piece of fatty, streaky bacon, cubed

salt and freshly ground black pepper

2 oven-ready wood pigeons

200g dark-gilled, open-cup mushrooms,
    quartered

1 large carrot, cut into thick slices

1 small onion, quartered

1 stick of celery, cut into short lengths

2 tbsp Cognac

250ml red wine

300ml chicken stock

3 cloves

1 bay leaf

6 juniper berries, bruised

1 heaped tsp redcurrant jelly

1 rounded tbsp flour

for the pastry

60g butter

60g lard

200g self-raising flour

pinch of salt

2–3 tbsp ice-cold water

1 egg, beaten

Now that I reconsider this pie, so relentlessly cooked, tested and most pleasurably scoffed, it occurs to me that it is, in fact, wood pigeons cooked in the style of a coq au vin, taken off the bone and put into a pie. Maybe not the most original of notions, but pastry and red wine pigeon gravy seems to be no bad thing, especially with that gorgeous gooey bit underneath the crust which is sogged by that particular gravy.

Note: you will need to cook the pigeon pie filling and allow it to cool, at least 4 hours before you assemble the pie; in fact, if you can, cook it the day before and store it, covered, in the fridge.

Preheat the oven to 140°C/275°F/gas mark 1.

Melt the butter in a large, heavy-based, lidded pot and in it quietly fry the bacon until crisp. Lift it out with a slotted spoon and put on a plate. Season the pigeons and slowly brown all over in the resultant bacon fat for several minutes, then remove and place alongside the bacon. Now tip in the mushrooms and fry them,

too, until well coloured. Also remove these and add to the pigeons and bacon. Add the carrot, onion and celery to the pot and fry them briskly in any remaining fat (add a touch more butter, if necessary) until slightly browned, before returning only the pigeons to the pot. Spoon over the Cognac, ignite it, then pour in the red wine and stock. Add the cloves, bay leaf, juniper and redcurrant jelly. Bring up to a simmer, put on the lid and braise in the oven for 1½ hours.

Lift out the pigeons, which will be good and tender, and carefully place back with the bacon and mushrooms. Strain the braising stock through a sieve suspended over a large saucepan, press the vegetable debris with a ladle to extract all flavour, then discard it. Now then, unorthodox as this may sound, sprinkle the flour over the surface of the stock – which will have a thin surface of fat upon it to absorb the flour – and vigorously whisk it in until dissolved. Bring this up to a simmer and allow to cook, quietly, for 10–15 minutes. Remove every scrap of meat from the pigeon carcases and add to the thickened stock. Tip in the reserved cooked mushrooms and bacon, mix in well, and continue cooking what has now become the pigeon pie filling, for a further half an hour. Tip into a bowl, leave to cool, then cover with clingfilm and put into the fridge for at least 4 hours, or overnight.

To make the pastry, cut the butter and lard into small chunks and place in a large bowl with the flour and salt. Gently rub the fat into the flour, using fingertips, until the texture resembles very coarse breadcrumbs. Mix in only just enough water to bind the mixture together. Lightly knead this dough until well amalgamated, dust with flour and slip into a plastic bag. Place in the fridge for 30 minutes before using.

Preheat the oven to 180°C/350°F/gas mark 4 and also place a flat baking sheet in there, which will help to cook the base of the pie more thoroughly. Lightly butter a loose-bottomed tart tin (approx. 20cm wide x 4cm deep). Roll out two-thirds of the pastry (not too thin) and use it to line the base and sides of the tin. Now roll out the remaining third to a similar thickness, and generously wide enough to use as a lid to the pie, and put to one side. Pile the cold pigeon mixture into the pastry-lined tin and lightly press it down.

Brush the edges of the pastry case with beaten egg to seal the pastry lid upon it, while also pressing the edges together lightly before trimming off any excess overhang. Brush the surface of the pie with more beaten egg, make 3 small incisions into the centre of the pie using the point of a sharp knife and, if you wish, further decorate the edges of the crust with the tines of a fork.

Bake the pie on the preheated baking tray on the middle shelf of the oven, for about 40–50 minutes or until the surface is a rich, golden brown. Remove from the oven and leave for a good 10 minutes before unmoulding and cutting into generous wedges. Eat with buttered Brussels sprouts or pickled red cabbage.

grilled squab pigeon with sweet sherry vinegar & shallot vinaigrette

serves 1

1 squab pigeon, or the French 'pigeonneau'
salt and freshly ground black pepper
a little extra virgin olive oil

1 very small shallot, very finely chopped
a trickle of PX (sweet) sherry vinegar
a squeeze of lemon juice (optional)

Another pigeon entirely, here. These are bred especially for the table and are, in fact, a type of dove. Have no fear, they are not the pretty white ones that live in dovecots. Moreover, most display similar plumage to the common pigeon that you might see in Trafalgar Square but, thankfully, are a little less scrawny and certainly better to eat. So cosseted, in fact, are these beautiful, corn-fed birds that their over-plump breasts almost make me blush. Be warned, however, they don't come cheap, so make the eating of these luxuries a special treat. By the way, the term 'squab' is the name mostly used for them in North America. In France, it is 'pigeonneau', as well as variations around the word 'palombe' in other European countries, such as Spain. And then there is that astonishing song 'Una Paloma Blanca': a white dove. Happy, now?

The sweet 'PX' sherry vinegar used here is a deliciously fragrant one made from Pedro Ximénez, a richly thick, sticky-sweet sherry of which, I must admit, I am none too fond as a drink. The resultant vinegar, however, is a star of my kitchen. Initially think balsamic vinegar, then instantly change your mind when you taste it.

Heat a ribbed, stove-top grill until medium hot. Take each side of the pigeon from the carcase using a small, sharp knife, keeping the knife hard against the breastbone structure. This will leave you with a breast and leg/thigh part in one complete half; ask your enterprising butcher to do this for you, if tentative. (Freeze the pigeon carcase for use in stock-making.)

Place the pigeon halves on a large plate and season well. Smear with a little olive oil, rubbing it into the skin. Place skin side down on the grill, while also balancing upon them a heavy pan, so keeping them flat while further allowing the skin to be attractively striped by the ridges of the grill. Cook for 5 minutes. Turn the birds over and grill for slightly less time on their skinless sides; the pigeon should be quite rare, at this stage. Now place the pigeon halves on a hot plate, sprinkle with the shallot and add the vinegar and a little more olive oil. Cover with a shallow bowl, or deep pan lid, say, and leave to rest for at least 5 minutes, by which time the shallots will have wilted slightly and the pigeon flesh become a nice rosy pink throughout.

Eat with a squeeze of lemon juice, if you like, accompanied by a few Cos salad leaves, taken from the heart of the lettuce; the juices and dressing from the squab will offer plenty of lubrication to these.

traditional English roast duck, with apple sauce

serves 4

1 x 2kg oven-ready duck, with giblets

salt and freshly ground black pepper

1 glass of white wine

2 carrots, peeled and chopped

1 onion, chopped

2 bay leaves

2 sprigs of thyme

½ a chicken stock cube

1 dsp redcurrant jelly

3 tbsp port

1 tsp potato flour, or arrowroot

watercress (optional)

for the apple sauce

2 small Bramley apples, peeled, cored
   and roughly chopped

4 cloves

1–2 tbsp caster sugar, to taste

squeeze of lemon juice

An Aylesbury duck, roasted and served with gravy and apple sauce, together with 'garden' peas, is a hotel dining-room dish that has not been seen since around the mid 1970s, I guess. Almost completely to blame, about a decade later, came the tentative trickle of imported duck breasts from France. Initially, it was only the 'magret de canard', the very large, fatty breast taken from a foie gras-producing duck, that was used. These were vacuum-packed, so possessing an excellent shelf-life and, furthermore, this 'sous-vide' process was soon to become one of the most exciting and profitable innovations of the time. Not surprisingly, the duck's shrink-wrapped legs swiftly followed suit, instantly turned into confit in every restaurant kitchen in the land, including mine.

So, in these days of easy breast and carefree confit, a proper English roast duckling (for genteel folk, this was the favoured description) is a truly scrumptious feast when carefully cooked – with hot, crisp skin and meltingly tender, well-cooked flesh beneath – and, for heaven's sake, very tasty! Well, you know what? I miss it very much indeed.

The exasperating result of the convenient duck portion has resulted in a sad decline of, all at once, roasting, carving and gravy-making skills. Simply, this is mainly due to an absence of carcase. For instance, I won't countenance the 'roasted' chicken or duck breast found on many restaurant menus as anything other than something ... well, something just cooked, actually. Yes, it may be placed in a small, heavy frying pan with added fat, then generously basted on the stove-top and roasted (flashed) in a very hot oven for about 5 minutes, but, essentially, it is nothing more than a sauté with a final, additional blast of wrap-around heat.

It is to the Chinese restaurant, of course, where one must now go to eat the finest roast duck. And, when push comes to shove, the Chinese are the finest duck-roasters of all. The Chinese method of pouring boiling water over the skin of a duck, then hanging it up to dry prior to roasting, is one of the best ways to achieve a crisp, dry skin. Another tradition, and not necessarily Chinese, is to first deftly puncture the skin all over many times with a thin skewer or the point of a sharp knife; and that is *just* under the skin, not gaily onward into the flesh, too. Anyway ... read on, if you wish to recreate the sound of that 70s duck, sizzling and roasting in a hot oven ...

As I like my apple sauce stone cold, I would make this first – even the day before, put into the fridge in a covered container. So, place the chopped apple in a small, stainless steel pan, add 4–5 tablespoons of water and then add the other ingredients. Place the pan over a medium heat and, once the mixture is beginning to bubble, allow to cook very slowly, stirring occasionally, until the apples have broken down to a sort of mush. When you have a rough sauce, and the sugar content pleases you, decant into a bowl to cool. Right then, to the duck ...

Remove the giblets from inside the duck, rinse them and put to one side, for later. Now, using a sharp skewer or the point of a very sharp knife, carefully prick the skin all over the breast and leg parts (not right through into the meat) until you tire of doing it, probably about 40–50 pricks in all. Now place the duck upon an inverted bowl, or similar and, within the confines of the sink, fully drench it all over – and on both sides – with boiling water poured directly upon it from a kettle.

You will now see that the tiny punctures you made will have opened up on contact with the boiling water, thus allowing the subcutaneous layer of fat beneath to later seep out as the duck cooks. The bird should then be allowed to dry. I find that the

best way to do this is to either rest it on a wire rack or hang it up on a meat hook; whichever method you choose, the close proximity of a breezy open window will enormously assist and speed up the process. About 3–4 hours should do, but overnight will give the finest results. In hot weather, however, this would not be an advisable procedure.

Preheat the oven to 230°C/450°F/gas mark 8.

Rub salt all over the duck's skin, then grind plenty of pepper inside the cavity. Now put the duck on a wire rack placed inside a roomy roasting tin and slide it into the oven. Roast for 30 minutes and then turn the temperature down to 180°C/350°F/gas mark 4. Roast for a further hour or so. No basting is required, but as the fat runs from the duck into the roasting tin, periodically pour it off into a metal bowl (keep this fat to roast potatoes). Once the roasting time is complete, remove the duck from the oven and allow to cool till warm and able to be handled. Leave the oven on.

Now, completely remove each half of the duck from its carcase using a small, sharp knife, keeping it close to the carcase as you work. Put the 2 duck halves back into the roasting tin (emptied of all traces of fat) and put to one side. Using a large, heavy knife, roughly chop and crush the carcase and put into a large pot. Add the duck giblets, also roughly chopped, together with the wine, vegetables and herbs. Pour in water to just cover, together with the half stock cube, redcurrant jelly and port. Bring up to a simmer, remove any scum from the surface and quietly cook for about an hour. Strain the resultant stock through a fine sieve into a clean pan (discard the solids) and reduce by at least half or, at least, until well-flavoured and very ducky. Slake the potato flour with a little water (or port) and slowly add to the stock until syrupy and of a gravy consistency. Turn up the oven to 200°C/400°F/gas mark 6.

Return the duck halves to the top of the oven and reheat for around about 20–25 minutes, or until the duck skin has become nicely crisp; you may flash them under a moderate grill, if you like, to aid final crisping. Carve into joints, present on a heated platter, and hand the gravy and apple sauce at table. Serve with watercress or peas – and I am particularly partial to fine-quality tinned ones, here – and some roast potatoes cooked in that collected duck fat.

slow-cooked rabbit in olive oil, with potatoes & aioli

··

serves 4, as a first course

shoulders, legs and belly of a
   farmed rabbit, chopped into
   similar-sized pieces: the legs into 3,
   the shoulders and belly in 2 (see below)

extra virgin olive oil

3–4 cloves of garlic

4–5 medium-sized waxy potatoes,
   scrubbed and washed

for the salting mixture

2 tbsp sea salt

2 tsp sugar

3–4 sprigs of thyme

1 bay leaf

10 black peppercorns

a generous grating of nutmeg

for the aioli

2 egg yolks

2 cloves of garlic, crushed to a paste
   with a little sea salt

freshly ground white pepper

300–350ml extra virgin olive oil

lemon juice, to taste

to serve

a little chopped parsley

··

If I were you, I would buy a whole, nicely farmed rabbit from an enterprising
butcher who will stock such an item. Ask him to joint it into two legs, two
shoulders, one trimmed saddle and the belly flaps removed from the latter.
This way, you can use everything but the saddle for the following dish and,
perhaps, roast the saddle a day or so later – or freeze it, well wrapped in
clingfilm for another occasion entirely.

    With regard to the quality of the olive oil, here, it is imperative that it is
very good indeed; so use your most favourite, special lotion – and, particularly
so, for the aioli.

    Note: the initial preparation for the rabbit needs attention the day before
it is cooked.

Put the ingredients for the salting mixture into a small food processor and whiz until fine. Place the rabbit joints in a shallow dish or lidded plastic container and pour over the salting mixture. Mix together with your hands until well coated, then put into the fridge for 24 hours, turning the rabbit occasionally.

The next day, rinse the rabbit in cold water and then leave to soak, covered in water, for about 1 hour, to remove excess salt. Preheat the oven to 140°C/275°F/gas mark 1.

Put the rabbit pieces into a deep, lidded pot which will accommodate them snugly. Pour over enough olive oil to just cover the rabbit, then tuck in the cloves of garlic. Just to allow the oil to start heating up, place the pot over a very low flame, stir the rabbit around a bit and, when there are a few bubbles beginning to show, cover the pot and put it into the oven. Leave to very slowly cook for about 1½ hours, or until the rabbit is starting to fall away from the bone, but leave a little longer if necessary; it is essential that the rabbit is well cooked.

When the rabbit is fully cooked, leave the pot to cool for about 15 minutes, then carefully lift out the rabbit and put it into a shallow dish until cool enough to handle. Strain the olive oil through a fine sieve into a bowl and discard any garlic or bits of rabbit debris from the sieve. Flake the pink and tender rabbit meat from its bones, put it into a lidded container and re-cover with the strained oil.

Note: I would not necessarily advise using the rabbit straight away as, like a confit, it is improved by at least a few days buried in fat/oil, in the fridge, where it may also be stored for at least a month. Once the rabbit meat has been used, keep the oil in the fridge for another occasion where you may like to repeat the dish. Or, use it to cook other things.

When you wish to serve the dish, steam (or boil) the potatoes in their skins. Take the rabbit flesh and warm it through in a pan with a little of its olive oil. Peel and thickly slice the potatoes, arrange on a platter and strew over the rabbit. Serve the dish warm, with the following aioli:

Place the egg yolks in a bowl with the crushed and salty garlic and the pepper. Beginning slowly, beat this together, while very, very slowly trickling in the olive oil. Once the mixture is becoming very thick, add a little lemon juice. Continue beating, adding the oil a little faster and increasing the speed a little. Taste as you continue beating, adding a touch more lemon juice and more seasoning as you think necessary. Once you are happy with the flavour and texture – which should be almost ointment-like – the aioli is ready.

roast teal with orange gravy

serves 2

2–3 oven-ready teal, according to size
a little oil
salt and freshly ground black pepper
2 tbsp port
1 tbsp Cognac
200ml chicken stock
1 tsp red wine vinegar

1 tbsp marmalade – the more
    orange-tasting the better
the juice and grated zest of 1 small orange
1 tsp potato flour, or arrowroot, slaked
    with very little water, or port
fresh orange segments, for decoration

A teal is the smallest of the wild duck family, as far as I know. A widgeon is slightly bigger, followed by the largest, the mallard, with the latter being the most common of all edible water fowls. All three are an acquired taste, in terms both of the faintest of fishy flavours and the fact that they can, occasionally, not be the most tender of birds. That said, a depth of flavour, together with a density of texture, makes them, for me, a seasonal and gamey treat. Teal can slightly vary in size, hence the suggestion (see above) that maybe three teal to serve two might be a generous option.

Preheat the oven to 220°C/425°F/gas mark 7.

Rub the teal with a smear of oil, then season them well. In a small and solid roasting tin (or heavy-based frying pan), cook them on the top shelf of the oven for 10 minutes, undisturbed. Remove and leave to rest for at least a further 10–15 minutes, or until cool enough to handle. As directed in the foregoing roast duck recipe (see page 190), remove the breast and leg/thigh parts from the teal so that you have 4 or 6 halves, and put to one side. Keep the oven on.

Roughly chop up the carcases and return to the roasting tin (or pan). On a moderate heat, stir these around until well crusted and also mixing with any bits that have stuck to the bottom of the tin. Add the port and Cognac and ignite them. Once the flames have died down, pour in the chicken stock and vinegar, then spoon in the marmalade. Add the orange juice and zest, stir everything together and allow to simmer for at least 30 minutes; if you wish, you could do this in the oven. You are, in effect, making teal gravy flavoured with orange, here.

Once you are happy with the flavour, strain this mess through a fine sieve into a small saucepan. Check for seasoning and then lightly thicken the gravy with the slaked potato flour (or arrowroot) until of a coating consistency, but take care not to over-thicken. Keep warm.

Return the teal halves to the roasting tin and put back into the oven. Reheat for no more than 5 minutes or so, once again, on the top shelf; they need to be pink. Once hot, place on 2 hot plates and spoon over the sauce. Garnish with the orange segments (the orange skin – and pith – removed with a small knife, then each segment cut and eased out from between the inner membrane) and serve forthwith. Very good indeed, accompanied by a purée of well-buttered celeriac root.

prawns
& shrimps
on toast,
a prawn salad
& a creamed
lobster

Irish creamed shrimps on butter-grilled toast

serves 4, for a sweet little Sunday supper

25g butter

a good scraping of nutmeg

pinch of ground mace

2 tbsp Irish whisky, Jameson's preferably

1 scant dsp anchovy essence

150ml double cream

200g peeled brown shrimps

4 slices of bread, taken from a plain
  white loaf

squeeze of lemon juice

1 tbsp finely chopped parsley

cayenne pepper

The 'Irish' in the name, here, simply refers to the whisky. However, I could easily envisage eating something like this in a cosy bar on the Galway coast, preceded, perhaps, by a plate of their excellent native oysters. Irish whisky, furthermore, is the only one that I enjoy; Scotch is too assertive for this Sassenach, and I particularly avoid a malt – however legendary its provenance or age. An occasional glass of Jameson's, however, is one that I love.

Note: it is now relatively easy to purchase plastic boxes of freshly peeled shrimps from good fishmongers, delicatessens and occasional supermarkets.

Using a small saucepan, melt the butter and add the spices and Irish whisky. Bring up to a simmer and ignite the mixture; there will be a small flame and, as you swirl the pan around, it will soon be extinguished. Now introduce the anchovy essence, allow to bubble for a few seconds and then stir in the cream. Bring up to a simmer and allow to thicken slightly and reduce. Tip in the shrimps, thoroughly heat through but do not overcook; the shrimps should be nicely coated with the sauce. Keep warm. To make the buttered toast, take four slices of white, crustless bread and thinly butter on both sides (use a sheet of greaseproof for turning over). Place under a grill and toast on both sides until crisp and golden.

Finally, stir a little lemon juice and the parsley into the creamed shrimps, pile them on the toast and lightly dust each serving with cayenne pepper.

chopped prawns, avocado & jalapeños, on toast

serves 2, as a luxury snack

Not so much a recipe as a thoroughly delicious assembly. I was, in fact, inspired to put these harmonious ingredients together by the man who snapped its pretty picture – and all the others, naturally, in this book – Mr Jason Lowe. He was wistfully relating to me how he used to make himself chopped avocado on toast (spread with Marmite as well!) as a fifteen-year-old teenager, the fruit picked from a tree which grew outside his study window at the school he attended in Zimbabwe. And what an endearing picture is evoked here.

This is the kind of toast topping that, frankly, does not need a list of measured ingredients; I certainly didn't weigh anything when I made it the first time. Simply take a fine, ripe *avocado*, peel it, and cut it into chunks. Place these in a bowl, squeeze over some *lime juice* (or lemon, if you have no lime to hand), and add a little *salt*. Now take a handful of some of those *cooked, shell-on prawns*, peel them and add to the avocado. Roughly slice a small green *jalapeño chilli* (some do, occasionally, turn red), seeds removed if you must, and also add to the avocado and prawns. Mix all well, tip out on to a board and strew over the mixture the leaves from a few sprigs of *coriander*. Take a heavy knife and chop all the ingredients together until a coarse purée; try to resist doing this in a processor, for it will become too smooth, especially the avocado. Return the mixture to the bowl, lubricate with a tiny trickle of *olive oil*, check for salt and more citrus juice, if needed, then pile on to a large slice of toasted rustic *bread* – sourdough, say – and spread thickly. Eat at once, cut into thick soldiers for ease of eating. Previously spread the toast with Marmite only if you are an addict ...

warm prawn salad with flageolet beans, onion, parsley & olive oil

serves 4, for a summery lunch out of doors

700–750g shell-on prawns, defrosted

2 tbsp tomato passata

1 tbsp red wine vinegar

1 small clove of garlic, crushed

salt and freshly ground black pepper

75–100ml extra virgin olive oil

600–700g cooked flageolet beans,
  drained weight, well rinsed

2 small tomatoes, peeled, seeded and
  finely chopped

1 medium red onion, very thinly sliced

3 tbsp chopped parsley

a little extra olive oil

Cooked, shell-on prawns are the ones to use here. These are available from most supermarkets and have been frozen, but the quality is good nonetheless. The contrast of the pale green beans together with the pink prawns is, I think, a winning collation.

Peel the prawns and remove their heads. Put the tail meat into a bowl and set aside. Using a small processor or liquidiser, whiz together the passata, vinegar, garlic and seasoning. Then, with the motor running slowly, start to incorporate the olive oil until creamy and homogenised; if it looks too thick, add a splash of warm water. Tip into a shallow pan, check for seasoning and piquancy, then add the beans and chopped tomatoes. Carefully stir together and warm through over a low heat.

Decant into a shallow serving dish, arrange the prawns and red onion on top, then liberally scatter with the parsley. Trickle over some extra oil and quietly mingle all the components together. Serve just as it is, with slices of grilled country bread.

lobster gratin

．．．

serves a couple of addictive,
  hard-working gourmets

1 x 500g cooked lobster, split in half
  lengthways, tail part thickly sliced,
  claw meat left in one piece

for the sauce
50g butter
1 tbsp olive oil
1 small onion, peeled and finely chopped
1 clove of garlic, crushed
1 small carrot, peeled and finely chopped
¼ of a small fennel bulb, finely chopped

shell debris from the cooked lobster,
  roughly chopped
salt and freshly ground black pepper
1 scant dsp tomato purée
generous splash of Cognac
generous splash of port
1 small glass of dry white wine
2 sprigs of fresh tarragon, chopped
250ml double cream
a small squeeze of lemon juice, to taste
1 egg yolk

．．．

Although the eating of this particular dish is quite sublime, the making of
it needs attention and not a little boisterous enthusiasm. Personally, and
when in the mood, I love to make this kind of rich little shellfish number,
but I understand that its origins lie in the professional kitchen, where much
simmering of chopped lobster carcases, flaming of Cognac and all that passing
and pressing through sieves, etc. is needed simply to fashion the sauce. In
essence, this is a dish you feel you really want to make, rather than merely
thinking about it. So, if that particular need is manifesting itself, go ahead.
However, if it all seems a bit too much trouble, then please choose to make
something else. Cooking a dish like this, after all, ought to be a pleasure.

   Note: if bothered by dealing with the lobster, ask a fishmonger to do it.
All body and claw meat needs to be removed, and also ask him to discard the
stomach sac, which lies in the head, as well as the thin intestinal tract.

To make the sauce, heat together the butter and olive oil and in it stew the
vegetables until softened. Add the lobster debris, seasoning and tomato purée and
stir in. Cook gently, stirring frequently, for a few minutes more, or until the tomato

purée has turned rust-coloured. Add the Cognac and port (ignite them if you wish), white wine and tarragon and bring to a simmer. Remove any froth that has been generated with occasional dabs from kitchen paper and then introduce the cream. Simmer very quietly for at least 30–40 minutes, then strain through a coarse sieve suspended over a clean pan, pressing down on the collected debris as much as you can with the back of a ladle, so forcing as much flavour through the sieve to collect below. Return this (now) sauce to a moderate heat and return to a simmer.

Preheat the oven to 220°C/425°F/gas mark 7.

As soon as the inevitable scum reappears once more on the surface, deftly remove it with a spoon. Allow to reduce and thicken before correcting the seasoning and adding a touch of lemon juice to taste. Finally, pass it through a very fine sieve and put to one side; its consistency should be that of double cream and it should taste richly of shellfish. Finally, add the egg yolk and thoroughly beat in until smooth.

Note: with regard to the addition of an egg yolk ... In restaurant kitchens, there is almost always hollandaise sauce lurking about somewhere and I have, in the past, used a little of that sauce in place of the egg yolk. If you were making this dish for a dinner party, say, then it would be well worth making some (see Smoked Haddock and Spinach, with Chive Butter Sauce, page 107); it offers an even more voluptuous finish to the sauce. Otherwise, stick with the simpler egg yolk.

To finish the dish, take 2 small ovenproof dishes, lightly butter them and lay in the lobster meat. Spoon over the sauce generously and slide the dishes on to the top shelf of the oven. Heat through for about 10 minutes, until the surface of the dishes has lightly burnished (put them under a hot grill for a finishing touch, if necessary). Serve at once, perhaps with some pilau rice.

two salmon,
a soaked
mackerel &
a butter
sauce for fish

fish (or shellfish) with a white butter sauce

....

serves 2

allow, per serving, say 150g salmon/
sea trout or white fish fillet, such
as turbot, brill or sea bass (200g if
the fish is on the bone, like the halibut);
4 large scallops, or 5, if medium sized;
½ a 750–800g lobster

for the white butter sauce (beurre blanc)
2 shallots, peeled and very finely chopped
4 tbsp white wine vinegar
4 tbsp white wine
4 tbsp water
250g cold, fine-quality unsalted butter,
    cut into small chunks
salt and freshly ground white pepper

....

This particular recipe is, to be honest, all about the wonderful white butter
sauce (beurre blanc), which goes so well with all kinds of fish. The first time
I enjoyed it was, naturally, in France, about forty years ago, served up with
a fine piece of wild salmon (for me its natural and most perfect partner).
The fish in the picture that you see accompanying the sauce (you see what
I mean: sauce comes first) is an equally fine halibut cutlet, simply because
on the day the dish was photographed, it was some super-fresh halibut that
won the day's fish shopping.

Apart from salmon and halibut, scallops are famously good with this
sauce. The relatively recent revival of a famous old Parisian Left Bank 'bistro
deluxe', chez Allard, does a particularly good version of St Jacques au beurre
blanc – or, at least, they did the last time I paid a visit. A split poached or
steamed lobster is also happy being bathed in a small ladleful of beurre
blanc. The fantastically expensive turbot is another thought for very special
occasions, or its cheaper cousin, brill. And a pale pink fillet lifted from a sea
trout (arriving in late spring) simply cries out for a little lubricating bb.

Note: a few words here regarding the sauce itself. I like the (very finely
chopped) shallots left in the sauce, although some prefer to sieve them out.
I think that to add cream negates the entire process, eventual taste and texture

of the emulsion; promoters of this – mild, it should be said – heresy say that it better 'holds' the sauce. Well, be that as it may. Mine always holds very well indeed, thank you. But – BUT! – those who choose to fry the shallots in olive oil at the commencement of the sauce ... well, I can only say that here be demons at work, culinary-wise. It is exactly that nuance of simmered raw shallots, quietly reducing and cooking away in nicely acidic liquids, that gives this legendary sauce its gentle charm. I rest my case.

To make the beurre blanc, mix together the shallots, vinegar, wine and water in a small, stainless steel pan. Allow this to reduce over a moderate heat until almost no liquid remains. Turn the heat down to very low indeed and then, using a small whisk, begin to incorporate the butter chunk by chunk, allowing each chunk to melt and homogenise before adding the next; it is also a good idea to occasionally take the pan off the heat, returning it when it is becoming too cool. Continue in this fashion until all the butter has been used up and the sauce has a pale and thin, custard-like consistency – and verging on that white butter look, to be truthful. Season, and keep warm on the side of the stove.

Whichever fish or shellfish you choose, cook it as simply as possible: scallops, briefly brushed with olive oil and quickly seared in a non-stick frying pan; halibut (as shown here), lightly cooked on a ribbed, stove-top grill; salmon or sea trout I always prefer steamed or poached; turbot or brill, steamed or lightly grilled. Oysters, drained of their juices (slurp these first), can also be very good flashed under a hot grill for a few moments, just to stiffen them, then napped with a spoon or two of beurre blanc. The most apt decoration, if you feel the need to pretty the dish, would be some finely snipped chives, naturally.

salmon cooked in spinach

....

serves 2

40g butter

1 small shallot, very finely chopped

2 tbsp dry vermouth

about 300g small spinach leaves

salt and freshly ground black pepper

a scraping of nutmeg

2 salmon fillets, approx. 300–350g in all

1 lemon, to serve

....

Here is a neat little dish that takes only a few minutes to prepare (and about time, you may well exclaim). It is also quite healthy.

Although I am using salmon fillets, here, you could also make the dish with salmon steaks or, even better, sections taken from a small, wild sea trout when in season, around the middle of May and continuing into early summer. Cook the sea trout on the bone and leave the skin intact, lifting it off once the fish is cooked; for fish cooked on the bone, allow a minute or two more cooking time.

Simply, take a large, solid-based, lidded pot and in it melt 25g of the butter over a medium heat. Add the shallot and soften it for a few minutes before pouring in the vermouth. Allow to bubble for a few moments, then tip in about a third of the spinach. Season lightly (don't overdo the salt, remembering that the spinach will wilt dramatically) and add nutmeg. Pop the salmon on top of the spinach, top up with the rest of the spinach, and add the remaining butter, in small flakes, on top. Put on the lid and reduce the heat to low. Allow the fish to 'steam' within the spinach leaves for about 7 minutes, then switch off the heat. Leave the lid intact for a further 7–10 minutes.

Remove the lid and push the spinach down into the pan, while also pushing it to one side, so revealing the pale pink salmon. Carefully retrieve the fish and put on to 2 warmed plates. Increase the heat under the spinach, stir it around vigorously, remove with a slotted spoon and pile alongside the salmon. Serve with the lemon to squeeze over the dish. Note: you may wish to somewhat reduce the liquid generated by the spinach juices, to add a more intense flavour while almost forming a sauce for the dish. However, do watch out for an increase in salt by virtue of this reduction.

salmon in pastry with currants & ginger, sauce messine

serves 2–3

for the pastry

120g cold butter

200g plain flour

pinch of salt

2–3 tbsp ice-cold water

for the salmon

2 globes of stem ginger in syrup, chopped

30g currants

90g softened butter

500g salmon fillet, centre cut, if possible

salt and freshly ground white pepper

1 small egg, beaten

for the sauce messine

2 egg yolks

1 tsp Dijon mustard

1 scant tbsp each of freshly chopped
  chervil, tarragon and parsley

2 shallots, very finely chopped

50g unsalted butter, softened

300ml double cream

juice of 1 small lemon

salt and a pinch of cayenne pepper

This old favourite of mine is a quite marvellous assembly, although some don't quite understand its charm. Apart from the fact that these detractors are wrong (ha!), they may also be unaware that it was originally offered to a discerning public when the great George Perry-Smith first put it on the menu at his legendary Hole in the Wall restaurant in Bath, some time during the early 1960s, if not before that (the restaurant, in fact, opened in 1952). With the pitch-perfect taste in food that this man had, he could not conceivably fashion something seen as tasteless.

For both my fortieth and fiftieth birthdays (celebrated together with my late, and dearest, best chum, the wine merchant Bill Baker), the Bristol-based cook Stephen Markwick (see the chapter on Cool Cucumber, etc., page 35) cooked enormous quantities of this particularly delicious salmon creation –

together with many other wonderful dishes too. Well, talk about the ecstatic reviews by over 100 guests, some of whom returned more than once to the salmon, saying … 'Oh, all right then, just another wafer-thin slice …'

To make the pastry, cut the butter into small chunks and place in a large bowl with the flour and salt. Gently rub the fat into the flour, using fingertips, until the texture resembles very coarse breadcrumbs (you may wish to use a food processor to do this, but watch out for initial overworking). Mix in just enough water to bind the mixture together. Lightly knead the dough until well amalgamated, dust with flour and slip into a plastic bag. Place in the fridge for 30 minutes before using.

Preheat the oven to 220°C/425°F/gas mark 7.

To make the sauce messine, first beat together the egg yolks and mustard in a bowl. Add the herbs, shallots, butter and cream and whisk together. Now place the bowl over gently simmering water and stir continuously until the sauce thickens to the consistency of custard. Squeeze in the lemon juice and season. Keep warm on the side of the stove, or over the hot water diluted with a little cold water, so that it is warm rather than hot, to avoid curdling the sauce.

In a small bowl, mix together the ginger, currants and softened butter. Cut the salmon into 2 equal pieces across the grain of the flesh, and season. Sandwich the two pieces together with the ginger/currant/butter mixture. Roll out the pastry until about 3–4mm thick (you may not need quite all of it, so freeze any remaining), place the salmon in the middle of it, then brush the beaten egg all around the exposed pastry. Fold the pastry over the fish, press together, and then carefully turn it over so that the seal is underneath. Brush the surface of this package with egg-wash, tuck in the ends, trim off any excess, then seal together with the tines of a fork.

Place on a lightly greased baking sheet and bake in the oven for 20–25 minutes, or until golden and crisp. Cut into thick slices using a sharp, serrated knife and serve with the sauce spooned alongside.

mackerel in white wine

serves 2

200–250ml dry white wine

2 tbsp tarragon vinegar

1 small carrot, very thinly sliced

1 small white onion, very thinly sliced

a few black peppercorns

½ tsp coriander seeds

2 large pinches of sea salt

a bay leaf, some parsley stalks,
 a sprig or two of thyme

pinch of sugar

2 spanking fresh mackerel, gutted
 and cleaned, heads removed

4–5 thin slices of lemon

A truly classic dish of the French repertoire, maquereau au vin blanc is mostly to be found on bistro or brasserie menus of the old school. However, it was once also a favourite dish prepared in the home, where a diligent mother would have purchased the finest, freshest summer mackerel from a market stall in a Norman or Breton fishing port. And let us hope that she still does such a thing. It is one of the simplest cold fish dishes to put together, rewarding the cook with a deeply tasty result: soft flakes of almost sweet-tasting fish, swimming in nicely aromatic juices. And so very inexpensive, too. Only use mackerel that are spanking fresh, for best results.

Preheat the oven to 180°C/350°F/gas mark 4.

Apart from the mackerel and lemon, put all the ingredients into a stainless steel pan and bring up to a simmer. Cook for 10–15 minutes, or until the carrot is almost cooked. Place the mackerel in a lidded dish where they will fit snugly. Lay the lemon slices over the fish and pour over the hot wine/vinegar liquid, including all its aromatics. Pop on the lid and cook in the oven for about 20 minutes, or until the mackerel are clearly cooked; test them with a small fork, carefully looking inside the cavity of the fish, where the flesh should be opaque and white. Leave to cool completely, then put into the fridge until needed. Personally, I like them really quite cold, but served with hot, small new potatoes (peeled, naturally), nicely buttered, and with lots of finely chopped parsley added too.

big cow,
little cow

the original Carpaccio

....

serves 4

approx. 500g piece of immaculately
   trimmed sirloin of beef
sea salt and freshly ground black pepper

for the mayonnaise
2 egg yolks
2 tsp smooth Dijon mustard
salt and freshly ground white pepper
300ml sunflower or other neutral oil

juice of ½ a large lemon
150ml light olive oil

for the sauce
150g homemade mayonnaise (see below)
1–2 tsp Worcestershire sauce
juice of ½ a small lemon, or a touch more
approx. 2 tbsp milk
salt and freshly ground white pepper

....

Here is Arrigo Cipriani talking about Carpaccio in *The Harry's Bar Cookbook* (Smith Gryphon, 1991): 'Carpaccio is the most popular dish served at Harry's Bar. It is named for Vittore Carpaccio, the Venetian Renaissance painter known for his use of brilliant reds and whites. My father invented this dish in 1950, the year of the great Carpaccio exhibition in Venice. The dish was inspired by the Contessa Amalia Nani Mocenigo, a frequent customer at Harry's Bar, whose doctor had placed her on a diet forbidding cooked meat.'

'Carpaccio,' Signor Cipriani goes on to say, '[which] has been copied by any number of good restaurants all over the world, is made by covering a plate with the thinnest possible slices of raw beef and garnishing it with shaved cheese or an olive oil dressing. The genius of my father's invention is his light, cream-coloured sauce that is drizzled over the meat in a crosshatch pattern.'

And how true. This original Carpaccio is, without doubt, a dish of genius. If you have never eaten the one in Venice, then why not try it at home. Here is how to do it. The following recipe is based upon the one served at Harry's Bar.

Note: I usually find that thinly sliced, not too well hung sirloin (nice and red, that is), trimmed of all fat and sinew and cut from a whole piece, is best, here. You will also need to make some mayonnaise for the base of the sauce. The recipe will yield more than you need, but it is always good to have some in the fridge. A hand-held electric mixer is best for the making of mayonnaise.

For the mayonnaise, put the egg yolks into a roomy bowl and mix in the mustard and some seasoning. Beginning slowly, beat together while very slowly trickling in the sunflower oil. Once the mixture is becoming very thick, add a little lemon juice. Continue beating, adding the oil a little faster now while also increasing the speed of the whisk. Once the oil has been exhausted, add some more lemon juice and then begin incorporating the olive oil. Once this has also been used up, add a final squeeze of lemon juice; the texture should be thick and unctuous. Taste for seasoning, then pack into a lidded plastic pot and keep in the fridge until ready to use.

Now you have the mayonnaise, you can make the Carpaccio sauce. Simply whisk all the ingredients together in a small bowl until pourable, but not too runny; the traditional look of the dish needs the cross-hatch pattern of the sauce to remain in place, not spreading out over the meat. On more than one occasion, in my kitchen, I have miscalculated the correct texture, so, as ever, practice makes perfect.

To serve the Carpaccio, slice the sirloin as thinly as you possibly can, using a thin, very sharp long knife. Place 1 slice of meat between a fold of waxed or greaseproof paper (or clingfilm), and gently beat thinner with, say, a rolling pin. Peel off the beef and arrange on a plain white, main-course size plate. Repeat this process and add to the first slice, pushing it up against the first one; 2–3 slices should be sufficient for one serving. Once you have a neat, roughly circular arrangement of meat, move on to the next plate, and so on. Finally, pour the sauce into a bottle and affix a pourer – of the type that you may use for a bottle of olive oil. Deftly, and swiftly, criss-cross the Carpaccio with the sauce, sprinkle on a touch of Maldon (for preference) sea salt and a brief grind from the pepper mill. Serve promptly. And I prefer to eat this just as it is; no further garnish necessary.

Incidentally, I once wrote about the Harry's Carpaccio in the *Independent* newspaper, about fifteen years ago now. The same Mr Jason Lowe took the pic for it then, with me banging on incessantly in the text about the red and white colours in the dish (see the Cipriani introduction). Blow me, can you believe that on this particular occasion a gremlin in the works of newspaper printing pulled a fast one: the picture emerged in black and white. Well... eventually, we laughed.

steak, kidney & potato pie

....

serves 4

for the pastry

150g lard, cut into small pieces then
   frozen for 10 minutes

250g plain flour

salt

3–4 tbsp iced water

for the filling

300g stewing steak, cut into 1cm dice

150g ox kidney, cut into similar-sized pieces

200g chopped onion

200g diced peeled potato

salt and plenty of freshly ground
   white pepper

1 tbsp plain flour

approx. 75ml cold water

a little milk, for glazing the pastry

....

A nod, here, to the kind of pie that I always wanted to grab and eat from
northern market stalls as a boy. The kind of individual pie of which I speak,
'Meat and Tatie Pie' ('tatie being potato, in the vernacular) smelt so very good
that I could easily have wolfed down two or three at nine in the morning, aged
ten. But, no. My dear, late mother would never have countenanced such
a thing. In the mildest, Hyacinth Bucket kind of way, we were not the kind
of family who bought meat and 'tatie pies from market stalls. Although
she bought every kind of finest fresh fish, vegetable, fruit, cheese and,
occasionally, black pudding from various favourite mongers, to purchase
something that was always proudly made by her at home, and to *her* mother's
recipe, was anathema. So it was not until about ten years ago that I first
bit into one.

    Well, I am here to tell you that they were absolutely fantastic. Warm and
juicy, the flakiest pastry, the whiff of onion somewhere, and so much white
pepper (ready-ground, naturally) in there it would catch your breath. Mum
made a big, deep pot of pie when moved so to do, but there was only ever a top
crust. Delicious as it most surely was – and I can taste it now – the best thing
about those individual market pies was the all-enveloping pastry: all top.
And sides. And bottom, too. The recipe that follows has this, but also some

kidney in it, too, which I think is rather nice. The lady of the house, however, may well have not approved …

You will need a loose-bottomed pastry tin measuring 4cm deep by 20cm wide, lightly greased. Also, a flat oven tray; to put into the oven to heat up, so that the base of the pie will cook through evenly.

To make the pastry, rub together the fat, flour and salt until it resembles coarse breadcrumbs. Quickly mix in the water and work together until you have a coherent mass. Knead lightly and put into a plastic bag. Leave to rest in the fridge until the filling has been prepared.

Preheat the oven to 200°C/400°F/gas mark 6.

Put all the ingredients for the filling – except the water and milk – into a roomy bowl and mix together well with your hands. Divide the pastry into two-thirds and one-third size pieces. Roll the larger piece into a circle about 3mm thick – it does not want to be too thin. Line the tin, leaving the overhang intact. Roll out the rest of the pastry for the lid and set aside. Pile the filling in right to the top and carefully pour in the water, which should only just reach the surface. Brush the edge of the overhanging pastry with milk and put on the lid. Press the edges together at the rim of the tin and then slice off the excess pastry with a knife.

Brush the surface with milk, then decorate and further press the edges together with the tines of a fork. Make 2 incisions in the centre of the pie and place on the tray in the oven. Cook for 25 minutes, then turn the temperature down to 150°C/300°F/gas mark 2. Bake for a further hour, checking from time to time that the pastry is not browning too much; if it is, loosely cover with a sheet of kitchen foil. Remove from the oven, allow to rest for 10 minutes, then cut into wedges. Very good indeed with pickled red cabbage or piccalilli.

beef tripe with spring onions, ginger, chillies & coriander

....

generously serves a healthy 2
 – who love tripe

5–6 dried shiitake mushrooms, left whole

800ml chicken stock

1kg beef tripe, cut into thick strips,
   briefly blanched in boiling water,
   then drained

200ml Shaohsing Chinese rice wine

75g fresh ginger, peeled and cut
   into thick slices

1 large onion, quartered

4 cloves of garlic, unpeeled and bruised

2 star anise

to finish the dish

2 small spring onions, trimmed and cut
   into slivers

1 thumb-size piece of fresh ginger, peeled
   and cut into thin matchsticks

1 mild green chilli, thinly sliced

1–2 tbsp coriander leaves, roughly chopped

a dash or two of light soy sauce, to taste

1 tsp cornflour or potato flour, slaked with
   a little rice wine (optional)

....

I really, really wish that more folk could get their head around the idea of eating tripe. Yes, it is an acquired taste: all at once of a deep and worryingly unusual fragrance, together with a texture that will be new to the uninitiated but, I hope, would grow into a favourite kind of bouncy tender.

And, what's more, I don't know any gourmet chums of mine who don't enjoy tripe. Oh, actually, no, there is just one, the chef and my friend Rowley Leigh. He ain't too fond of it, nor does he enjoy the extra-deep taste of a French andouillette, that 'whiff of the farmyard' tripe sausage that can rift a lunch table into those who do and those who can't at all contemplate this rude food. Tripe is also supposed to be good for you, but that will always be secondary to the texture and flavour for me.

In London, I buy my beef tripe from two purveyors. The most convenient for me is in Shepherd's Bush market, which boasts a few halal butchers, all of

which sell tripe in various forms; there is even goat tripe in one of them. The other place I visit is a Chinese supermarket in Lisle Street, Chinatown, in London's West End. Here, they sell packets of frozen tripe, one labelled 'manifold', the other 'honeycombe', with the latter being the most commonly recognised type. I usually buy one of each, if up West.

Put the shiitake mushrooms in a bowl, then boil a ladle or two of the chicken stock and pour it over them. Leave to soak for 30 minutes. Put the tripe into a solid-based lidded pot, add the rice wine, the mushrooms (with their stock), the rest of the chicken stock, the ginger, onion, garlic and star anise. Stir together, bring up to a very quiet simmer and cook for at least 2 hours, or until very tender indeed (you could cook the tripe in a very low oven, if you prefer, at 140°C/275°F/gas mark 1).

Using a slotted spoon, lift out the tripe and put it into another pan. Strain the cooking liquor over it and discard all debris. Reheat the tripe and add the finishing spring onions, ginger, chilli and coriander leaves. Season with a little soy sauce and, if you think it necessary, very lightly thicken the sauce with the slaked cornflour (or potato flour). Serve at once, with plainly boiled rice.

oxtail 'nehari' with potatoes

···

serves 2–3

1kg oxtail joints, about 8 pieces, say

plain flour

50g butter or ghee

500g onions, thinly sliced

4 cloves of garlic, sliced

1 sachet of nehari spice mix (50g – but if
   you wish for a milder curry, just add
   a bit less)

500ml water

75g creamed coconut

10–12 curry leaves (optional)

300g cherry tomatoes

600g waxy potatoes (medium-sized
   Desiree are good), peeled and cut
   into chunks

a little fresh coriander, chopped (optional)

···

A little over two years ago, I was taken by friends to the Lahore Kebab House, just off Commercial Road in London's East End. I had long heard of this place and how basic it was. Full marks there: formica tables, strip lighting and absurdly tiny paper napkins; as I always get so messy with Indian food, I despatched about twenty, I reckon. Anyway, such piddling details ... More importantly, I was also promised that the food tasted wonderful. And so it did.

The finest dish of all, by far (though none were less than good and we ate for England) was a lamb shank 'nehari'. This was a favourite of one friend, who assured me of its very particular, aromatic heat and superb gravy – of which there was copious amounts; so very good indeed it turned out to be that I found myself finishing it with a spoon, as soup. Just marvellous meat, too, so yielding and soft, falling off the bone in fondant lumps.

I was so impressed by the lamb nehari that I asked of the restaurant manager the blend of spices – I knew I could detect aniseed in there some-where, at least. So he scuttled off to ask in the kitchen and returned with a colourful, cardboard packet. Well, although pleased indeed that I would easily be able to replicate this nehari at home, I was privately amused over the original idea that all the grinding and careful mixing of spices by the Lahore kitchen was so swiftly cast to the wind. And, by the way, in case you are wondering, I decided to use oxtail in the following recipe mainly because the price of lamb shanks on the day was of a similar price to a leg of lamb! Oxtail was half the price – and is every bit as tasty here, too.

To buy a packet of Laziza nehari masala mix, either go to a good Asian supermarket or look online, where an excellent and entire range of super-fresh, vacuum-packed spice mixes is at your disposal.

Note: other brands that manufacture nehari masala mixes have, so far, come nowhere near the fragrance and heat of the Laziza brand. But that which really appeals to me, here, is that I can make a very good, particular curry without constantly updating individual spices, which so very quickly become stale.

One final note: do not add salt to the dish, as the spice mix includes this. And don't follow the recipe on the packet; follow mine.

Preheat the oven to 150°C/300°F/gas mark 2.

Generously coat the oxtail with flour. Melt the butter (or ghee) in a large, lidded pot and fry the joints until golden brown. Remove the meat and tip in the onions. Fry these until softened and starting to colour. Add the garlic and continue to cook both for a further 5 minutes, or so. Sprinkle in the nehari spice mix and stir in, then cook the spice for a further 2–3 minutes. Pour in the water, bring up to a simmer and add the coconut, stirring it around until it has dissolved. Return the oxtail to the pot, bring back to a simmer and add the curry leaves if you have some. Put on the lid and cook in the oven for 1½ hours.

Remove from the oven and remove any excess fat from the surface using several sheets of kitchen paper; there will be more fat than you think, but leave a little behind for that authentic 'curry' look. Now add the tomatoes and potatoes and stir them in. Bring back to a simmer, cover once more and return to the oven. Cook for a further 45 minutes to 1 hour, or until the potatoes are tender. Finally, stir in some chopped coriander, if using. Serve with some plain and fragrant, steamed basmati rice if you wish, but I am quite happy only to have the potatoes, as starch.

veal

fillet of veal with anchovy mayonnaise & asparagus

....

serves 4, as a first course

16–20 asparagus, depending on size,
   trimmed and partially peeled

for cooking the veal

approx. 450g veal fillet, well trimmed,
   to give a weight of around 375g

salt and freshly ground black pepper

2 tbsp olive oil

4–5 tbsp dry vermouth

juice of ½ a small lemon

2 cloves of garlic, bruised

1 sprig of rosemary, broken in half

for the anchovy mayonnaise

4 tbsp homemade mayonnaise
   (see Carpaccio recipe, page 225)

4 anchovies, chopped almost to a paste
   (or use a small processor, together
   with the mayonnaise)

squeeze of lemon juice, to taste

pinch or 2 of cayenne pepper

....

One word of warning here: veal fillet is not exactly cheap. However, it is a most gorgeous cut, so tender, so pale pink and soft. I never understand, in fact, when so-called experts talk of meat, that a beef fillet steak, say, should be eschewed in favour of other cuts simply because it has less flavour and is only about tenderness. Well, geddaway. Of course it is! I mean, I love rump, sirloin, bavette and other, less tender cuts, too, but it entirely depends on what I feel like cooking and eating. A small fillet steak is a lovely thing, easy on the mouth and, when judiciously seasoned and quietly cooked in butter, remains one of my most favourite things to eat.

Actually, there is no doubt in my mind that the stumbling block here is cost. As an example, exactly the same misguided opinion applies to those who often say that they prefer crab to lobster. 'Oh, do you now?' I say. 'And why is that?' The usual reply is that it has more flavour. Poppycock. Quite simply, these are two completely different shellfish, absolutely wonderful to eat in their own particular way. But it is always that niggling cost, disguised as some gastronomic preference. To take the point to an almost surreal analogy, I have yet to hear anyone say that they would rather eat a carrot than a parsnip (assuming one enjoys both, that is).

Ah well, irritable cook aside … Just enjoy costly and special things once in a while, as a treat. Having said all of that, you could always use a pork fillet here, if you want; and no, not quite the same, but a tasty alternative. Finally, if you are a fan of vitello tonnato, the Italian way with thinly sliced, cold veal and tuna sauce, the following marriage of flavours will be familiar to you.

Season the fillet of veal, then heat the olive oil in a heavy-based, lidded pot and quietly seal the meat on all sides, but only until pale golden, not at all browned. Add 1 tablespoon of vermouth, a squeeze of lemon juice and allow to bubble. Introduce the garlic and rosemary, partially cover the pot, and very, very gently braise the veal, while occasionally basting, for about 5 minutes. Turn the meat over, add a little more vermouth and lemon juice, then cook for a further 5 minutes. Do this perhaps twice more, turning the meat each time, and maybe sometimes without the lid, until the vermouth and lemon juice have reduced until syrupy, while also nicely coating the veal; total cooking time about 20–25 minutes. Remove the veal to a cold dish, (discard the garlic and rosemary) together with every vestige of juice, and cover with kitchen foil. Note: this method will give you a piece of very pink meat and, as the veal will now be left to completely cool, it will emerge just the rarer side of pale pink, once sliced.

To make the anchovy mayonnaise, simply mix the ingredients together until smooth.

To serve, slice the veal thinly, put on to 4 plates and spoon some of the anchovy sauce alongside. Cook the asparagus in fiercely boiling, salted water until tender – and not too crunchy, please. Drain the asparagus well, and arrange some on each plate. Trickle with a little of the veal cooking juices, together with some extra olive oil, if you like, and grind over a little black pepper to finish. The contrast of the cold veal, the salty-fishy mayonnaise and the hot asparagus is, if I might say, a luxuriously simple assembly.

grilled veal chop with ceps, parsley & garlic

serves 2

2 veal chops

salt and freshly ground black pepper

olive oil

1 lemon, to serve

for the ceps

2 tbsp olive oil

100g fresh ceps, cleaned and thinly sliced

salt and freshly ground black pepper

25g butter

2 cloves of garlic and the leaves from
  4 or 5 sprigs of parsley, finely chopped
  together (persillade)

What can I say? Here is a combination of such perfection – and really nothing to do with me – that it beggars belief. Grilled, succulent and pink veal, the finest wild mushroom known to man (don't argue), chopped garlic and parsley. And that is it. You could do the thing using dried ceps, reconstituted in warm water, then drained, but I urge you to buy these some time in the very late summer-into-autumn, when occasional foraging is going on somewhere near you.

Heat a ribbed, stove-top grill until hot. Season the chops, brush them with a little olive oil and place on the grill. Cook for about 5–7 minutes on each side, until nicely marked from the grill – a good golden brown with a nicely pink interior is perfect. Leave them to rest in a warm place while you quickly cook the ceps.

Heat the olive oil in a large frying pan (non-stick is good, here) until moderately hot. Throw in the ceps, toss them around in the oil and add just a touch of salt and pepper. Cook them briskly with the aid of a wooden spoon, to both keep them separate and take on a little colour at the same time. Add the butter, turn up the heat a touch and allow it to sizzle. Only now throw in the garlic and parsley, toss around to mix and then immediately spoon over the chops. Hand a cut lemon at table for squeezing over, if you wish.

calf's liver with sweet & sour onions

....

serves 2

2 red onions, very thinly sliced

2 tbsp olive oil

25g butter

salt and freshly ground black pepper

4 thin slices of calf's liver, cut into
   thin strips

1 tbsp sherry vinegar, or excellent-quality
   red wine vinegar

1 tbsp crème de cassis
   (a mildly alcoholic blackcurrant cordial)

1 tbsp chopped parsley

....

In its finishing moments, this is a quick dish. Just make sure that you take time to cook the slow beginning: the onions. Most important, this bit, for you need them to be very, very soft and sweet before you add the flash-in-the-pan liver, so keeping it nice and pink within. If you like, and when in the mood, you may cook the onions way in advance, just warming them through before you assemble the final fry-up.

In a heavy-based, preferably non-stick frying pan, cook the onions in 1 tablespoon of the olive oil and all the butter until completely cooked through and soft. They may take on a little colour during this time but no matter; the most important thing is that they cook slowly – up to 30 minutes, if necessary. Season lightly with salt and pepper, then tip out into a bowl and put to one side. Wash and dry the frying pan.

Heat the remaining olive oil in the frying pan until hot. Season the calf's liver with salt and pepper and briefly fry for 20 seconds, while also briskly tossing the liver around until just stiffened. Add to the onions in the bowl, thoroughly mix them together and return to the pan. Quickly heat through and add the vinegar, crème de cassis and parsley. Spoon on to hot plates and serve at once. Very good with softly creamed potatoes, or some equally soft and buttery polenta.

which whizzes itself into the utmost smoothity before you can say Magimix. Because I have been cooking for some time now, I don't find it any trouble forming the traditional 'quenelle' shape, fashioned by moulding it between two spoons until egg-shaped. And, if you look closely, you will see that this is how they are presented in the related photograph illustrating the dish. However – and without being in the least patronising – I have instructed that you should use either dariole moulds or ramekins, lightly buttered and cooked quietly in a bain-marie (or steamed, if you wish), at a low oven temperature until just set. If you wish, you might enjoy doing the quenelle thing, which involves the aforementioned spooning process, then dropping them into just simmering (shuddering is a better description), salted water until set. Have a go. You know you want to.

Note: if the scallops come with roes you could fry these in a little butter and garnish the mousses with them. I have also asked for the cream to be weighed as, if you have one of those scales that reverts to zero at the touch of a button, it is so simple to place the bowl of the processor directly on the scales when you first weigh the scallops, then again when you introduce the cream to them, once puréed. Finally, please place the components (but not the motor, obviously) of a food processor in the freezer for 20 minutes before using, as this keeps everything nice and cool while processing; delicate fish can easily begin to 'cook' when overworked, and cream is liable to curdle for the same reasons.

Place the scallops and egg in the chilled food processor and briefly work until very smooth. Place in the fridge (not freezer), still in the processor bowl, for 10 minutes. Return to the machine, begin to break down the scallop purée, and then add the cream. Process once more, until thoroughly blended with no streaks of scallop visible. Only now add the salt and cayenne, briefly mixing them in. You will see that the mixture begins to noticeably thicken, due to the salt; don't ask me why, it just does. Decant the mousse into a bowl, cover with clingfilm and put into the fridge.

To make the duxelles, fry the shallots in the butter until pale golden, then add the mushrooms. Season and stew together until fairly dry and any juices from the mushrooms have been driven off. Add the vermouth and simmer until reduced to almost nothing. Squeeze in the lemon juice, add the parsley and then briefly work in a small food processor, using the pulse button, until the mixture becomes an even purée – but it should not be over-smooth. Tip into a bowl, cover with a plate and keep warm over a pan of simmering water.

Preheat the oven to 170°C/325°F/gas mark 3.

For the mornay sauce, take a small saucepan and in it melt the butter. Tip in the flour, stir it around and cook quietly for a few minutes without colouring the mixture (roux). Pour in the milk all in one go and whisk together vigorously until smooth. Cook over a very low heat, stirring now with a wooden spoon, for about 7 minutes, until the sauce has thickened. Now add the Gruyère and stir in until melted, together with the cream if you wish for a slightly richer sauce, and cook for a further 5 minutes or so. Season lightly with salt, pepper and nutmeg, then put on a lid and also keep warm.

Lightly butter 4 dariole moulds or ramekins. Fill with the scallop mousse and smooth the surface. Cover each with a small square of buttered kitchen foil and place in a deep roasting tin. Pour tap-hot water around the moulds/ramekins and slide the tin into the oven. Bake for 20 minutes, or until the mousses feel set – only just bouncy – when tentatively pressed with a finger. Heat an overhead grill to medium-hot.

To assemble and finish the dish, take 4 shallow, ovenproof dishes and lightly butter. Take about a tablespoon or so of the mushroom duxelles and spread into the dish, forming a small, flat circle, roughly the diameter of the top of the mousses. Invert a mousse on to the duxelles and spoon enough mornay sauce over each one so that it is completely covered and with a little sauce running around them in the base of the dishes. Sprinkle each one with a light dusting of Parmesan, then put under the grill until lightly glazed and pale golden. Serve forthwith. Just delicious.

scallop & parsley soup

serves 4, delicately

50g butter

2 leeks, white parts only, sliced and rinsed

2 bunches of parsley (large,
   supermarket size, either flat or curly
   varieties), stalks and leaves separated,
   stalks roughly chopped

1 large baking-size potato, peeled
   and chopped

750ml chicken stock

salt and freshly ground white pepper

150ml double cream

150g scallops, diced small

This is based upon a recipe I used to make years ago, involving Jerusalem artichokes. No more, sadly, as these very agreeable and delicious tubers no longer agree with me; the wind generated would lift a Zeppelin. The charm of this soup is further enhanced by its gorgeous green colour.

Melt the butter in a stainless steel pan and sweat the leeks and all the parsley stalks gently, uncovered, for 20 minutes. Add the potato and chicken stock, salt and pepper and simmer quietly for a further 30 minutes, or until the potatoes are very tender. Coarsely chop the leaves of 1 bunch of parsley and add to the soup. Simmer for 5 minutes. Meanwhile, blanch the leaves of the other bunch of parsley in fiercely boiling water for 30 seconds. Drain and refresh immediately under cold running water, then gently squeeze dry in a tea-towel.

Liquidise the soup with the blanched parsley until smooth. Pass through a fine sieve into a clean pan, whisk in the cream and bring up to a simmer. Just before it reaches that point, add the diced scallops and cook through until just firm, about a minute; eat a bit, just to check, as they cook very quickly. Pour into heated bowls and serve at once. Very nice indeed with small, buttery croutons handed at table.

mussels

mussels with Gewürztraminer & cream

serves 2, generously

75g butter

2 medium onions, peeled and finely chopped

2 cloves of garlic, finely chopped

½ a bottle of Alsatian Gewürztraminer

2kg mussels, cleaned and de-bearded

½ tbsp finely snipped chives

1 tbsp finely chopped parsley

freshly ground white pepper

4 tbsp double cream

The unique taste of an Alsatian Gewürztraminer is just the ticket when cooking mussels. Its fragrance – the smell of lychees always comes to mind – has a particular affinity with the sweet and salty shellfish, producing a sauce of the utmost savour. The chef at Bibendum, Matthew Harris, put me on to this idea, so many thanks to him.

Note: as usual, do not use any mussels that refuse to close when raw; also, any mussels remaining closed, once cooked, discard.

Take a very large pan that has a lid. Melt the butter and in it fry the onions until softened, then add the garlic and cook for a minute or two more. Pour in the wine and allow to come to the boil. Tip in the mussels, put on the lid and, holding the pan in both hands, shake it around a bit. Put on a high heat and cook for 2 minutes. Lift off the lid, have a look to see how the mussels are doing and give them another shake, attempting to bring the opened ones on the bottom up to the top. Place back on the heat, put on the lid and continue cooking for a further minute or two. When it seems that all the shells are fully open, tip in the chives and parsley, some pepper and, finally, the cream. Shake and stir around for the last time, then tip into a large, hot bowl. It goes without saying that you will need some best bread, here, as you dig in and eat.

mussels 'Rockefeller' style

serves 2, as a first course

for the mussels

30g butter

2 small shallots, finely chopped

1 stick of celery, peeled and chopped

1kg mussels, cleaned and de-bearded

2 tbsp pastis (Pernod or Ricard)

200ml dry sherry

for the Rockefeller mixture

200g spinach (blanched in boiling, lightly salted water, rinsed under cold running water, drained and squeezed dry)

40g butter

10g parsley leaves

leaves from 2 sprigs of tarragon

2–3 healthy slugs of Tabasco sauce

I had always wanted to try to do mussels Rockefeller, in the same way as one would do the same for the classic recipe for oysters, originally hailing from the legendary restaurant Antoine's, in New Orleans. The original recipe from there is, apparently, a closely guarded secret but, along the way, it emerged from somewhere because I managed to include a version in my book *Gammon and Spinach* (Macmillan 1998). The recipe was originally given to me by my friend Gay Bilson, the Australian cook, author and intellectual, who is now rightly regarded as one of that country's living national treasures.

If you are familiar with how oysters Rockefeller are made – in essence, a pungent spinach purée spread on top of oysters, then baked – you will understand that to do this to dozens of small mussels would become an endless, tedious affair; I guess that if one could obtain some of those large Spanish mussels, the idea might just work, but I haven't seen these in the UK for years.

So, still wishing to marry the lovely aniseed flavours of this spinach purée with mussels, I decided to turn it into a sauce – and jolly nice it is, too, if a touch messy to eat; have fingerbowls to hand, for the fussy.

Note: as usual, do not use any mussels that refuse to close, when raw; also, any mussels remaining closed, once cooked, discard.

Melt the butter in a large pot (large enough to eventually accommodate the mussels) and in it quietly fry the shallots and celery until softened. Tip in the mussels, increase the heat until the sound of sizzling emanates from beneath, then add the pastis, which will seethe. Ignite it (stand back) and, when the flames have died, pour in the sherry. When steam is rising from the base of the pot, give the mussels a shake, trying to bring the opened ones on the bottom up to the top. Place back on the heat, put on a lid and continue cooking for a further minute or two. When it seems that all the shells are fully open, immediately strain into a colander suspended over a bowl. Shake the mussels about a bit, so extracting all clinging juices, then put them to one side. Also, keep the pot to hand.

Now, pour the juices into a liquidiser (or processor) and add all the ingredients for the Rockefeller mixture. Whiz until smooth and return this (now) green sauce to the mussel-cooking pot. Remove the empty half shells from the mussels and return the full halves to the green sauce. Briefly reheat and serve with thick slices of either toasted baguette or sourdough.

potato &
pulse

potato

potato soup with soured cream & chives

serves 4

25g butter

5 rashers of fatty, smoked streaky bacon (optional)

1 large onion, chopped

1 litre light chicken stock

500g floury potatoes, peeled and cut into chunks, and of a variety that will collapse when you boil them

salt and freshly ground white pepper

1 bay leaf

4–5 tbsp soured cream (not crème fraîche)

1–2 tbsp snipped chives

The inclusion of bacon in the soup, here, is a matter for you. Obviously, if vegetarian (also substitute vegetable stock, if so) or you are not allowed bacon, then it has to go. However, it does impart a lovely flavour to the soup, a nuance if you like, and it is not evident in itself once the soup is served.

The texture here is far nicer when put through a hand-cranked vegetable mill (mouli-légumes). As well as that attribute, a blender can often turn potato-based soups gluey. I would also like to mention that although many think that cultured crème fraîche is almost the same as soured cream, it is not. The texture of soured cream is softer, for one thing (better for melting into the soup), being less rich. And the flavour is more correct here, too: the perfect foil for chives, as always.

Melt the butter in a pan and add the bacon. Cook it gently until golden, then remove to a plate. Add the onion and stew until soft. Pour in the stock, then add the potatoes, seasoning and bay leaf. Bring up to a gentle simmer, skimming off any scum that forms on the surface, and reintroduce the bacon. Cook quietly for about 25–30 minutes, or until the potatoes break up a bit, when poked. Remove the bay leaf and bacon (keep in the fridge and grill until crisp for a bacon sandwich the following morning), then pass through a vegetable mill (mouli-légumes), using the finest mesh disc, into a clean pan. Gently reheat and ladle into hot bowls. Serve with a good dollop of soured cream and sprinkle with plenty of chives.

potato gnocchi with butter, sage, garlic & pine kernels

serves 4

100g butter

2–3 cloves of garlic, peeled and sliced

1 tbsp pine kernels

about 20 sage leaves

freshly ground black pepper

2–3 tbsp freshly grated Parmesan

for the gnocchi

500g potatoes, not too floury (Desiree
are good, or the less well-known
Belle de Fontenay; see below), unpeeled

1 egg, beaten

200g plain flour, plus a little more for
rolling only if necessary

½ tsp salt

The finest gnocchi I have ever eaten were those made by Toni Vianello, when he was cooking at his place in Paris, L'Osteria, in Le Marais. As far as I understand, he is no longer there, but I hope that the gnocchi remain as good, whoever is cooking there now. Toni once allowed me to watch them being made, but I have never been able to achieve their exquisite lightness and almost fudgy interior.

The amount of flour given here is a maximum amount, so don't use all of it if you feel that the texture needs no more; practice and experience makes for perfect gnocchi. I still have trouble from time to time, which is mainly due, I believe, to the age, variety and texture of the potatoes. I have a vague memory of Toni using large Belle de Fontenay potatoes, and storing them in a cool, dark place for some time before use, so that they dried out somewhat – which makes sense: excess moisture is the enemy of fine gnocchi.

Steam (or simmer) the potatoes in their skins until tender. Once cool enough to handle, peel them and then directly put through a potato ricer (favourite) or vegetable mill (mouli-légumes) on to a lightly floured kitchen surface. Allow to cool, then loosely gather the potato together and make a well in the middle with your fingers. Drop in the egg and sift over the flour with the salt. Now gently bring everything together using your hands and knead deftly to a soft dough. At this stage you may need a little more flour, both on the surface and in the mixture. The correct consistency should be similar to soft pastry.

Now roll the dough into long sausage shapes about 2.5cm in diameter, and cut into 2cm pieces. Dust lightly with sifted flour and put on a tray. Refrigerate for 30 minutes, then begin to shape them. Take a fork and, holding it in the left hand, prongs pointing uppermost, pick up one of the pieces of dough. Using your thumb, push the dough down the prongs to make a ridged surface, while simultaneously flicking each piece (a gnocchi) off the tines on to the work surface; this will also form a depression on the other side from your thumb. Once the gnocchi are formed, return them to the floured tray.

Bring a large pan of unsalted water to the boil and drop in about a third of the gnocchi. Simmer until they float to the surface, then give them a further 20–30 seconds. Lift out with a slotted spoon, drain well and place in a heated dish, together with a scrap of butter. Keep warm, cooking the remaining gnocchi in 2 further batches.

Melt the butter with the garlic slices and pine kernels and cook until pale golden. Remove them to a plate, then add the sage leaves to the butter, allowing them to froth and crisp up. Return the garlic and pine kernels. Spoon this buttery mass over the gnocchi, grind over plenty of black pepper and dust with Parmesan. Serve without delay, on hot plates, handing extra Parmesan at table.

best potato salad

serves 4

700g potatoes, unpeeled
2 tbsp chopped spring onions
1 tbsp finely chopped parsley

for the dressing

2 tbsp smooth Dijon mustard
2 tbsp red wine vinegar
salt and freshly ground black pepper
a small jug of warm water
325ml sunflower, groundnut or
    other neutral oil

The most important thing to remember when making a fine potato salad is to add the dressing while the potatoes are still warm. And please, please, *please* use peeled potatoes. You may follow the instructions given below, peeling the potatoes once cooked, or peel them from raw, but there is absolutely nothing worse than irritating little bits of potato skin in a potato salad, getting stuck in your teeth and ruining the entire, luscious assembly.

One of the most bizarre memories of potato-skin incidents occurred about a decade ago, when I had been stood up for a lunch at a grand, London West End hotel dining room. I decided to have my lunch anyway, sitting happily and solitary at a generous-sized table; it was, after all, to have accommodated two. Well, it was early June, with Jersey Royal potatoes in all the shops everywhere. And what was I given with my roast saddle of spring lamb from the trolley? Imported new potatoes, thin and papery skins fully attached. As I sat there, patiently peeling the skin from my own potatoes on to a side plate, not one waiter approached to ask if I was quite happy getting on with this kitchen task. Oh yes, there were occasional strange looks *en passant*, but not the slightest suggestion of this chore being given to a commis chef, rather than a paying guest. An astonishing occasion, to be sure.

Note: you will probably have some of the salad dressing left over, so store it in a screw-top jar in the fridge where it will keep happily for several days or longer; it is just easier to make the dressing in a larger quantity than you might necessarily need.

To make the dressing, put the mustard, vinegar, seasoning and a couple of tablespoons of the warm water into a small blender or food processor. Process until smooth and then start adding the oil in a thin stream. When the consistency is creamy, have a taste. If you think it is too thick, add a little more water; the consistency should be one of thin salad cream.

Put the potatoes to simmer in salted water. When evenly cooked through, drain and leave until you are able to handle them, then peel; peeling potatoes while still warm is easier and, furthermore, warm potatoes soak up the dressing much better than cold ones. Slice or roughly cut the potatoes into a warm dish, sprinkle over the spring onions and parsley, then spoon over the dressing and mix together quickly, while still warm.

I find that I can always eat this salad just as it is. However, it is also very lovely with cold and hot ham, rare beef, salmon – all kinds of cold cuts, in fact.

split peas & ham hock

serves 4

for cooking the ham hocks

2 small ham hocks (approx. 1.75–2kg
  total weight)

2 large leeks, trimmed, split and washed

2 sticks of celery, each cut in half

2 carrots, sliced lengthways

2 onions, 1 stuck with 4 cloves

2 bay leaves

a few peppercorns

250ml dry cider

for cooking the split peas

350g green split peas, soaked in cold
  water for about 2 hours

12 small carrots (Chantenay are nice, here),
  peeled and left whole

2–3 leeks, trimmed and cut into 6cm
  lengths

50g butter

salt and freshly ground white pepper

3 tbsp chopped parsley

I adore split peas: their mealy texture, easy absorption of other flavours and, frugally, how nicely inexpensive they are. They also, of course, make fabulous soup. So, with this in mind, I have hopefully made provision for there to be enough leftover broth, peas and ham to make this gloriously warming brew (see the following recipe).

There are two sets of vegetables employed here. I used to think that the vegetables included while the ham hocks are cooking would be just fine to eat when the dish was ready. However, I soon began to tire of their tired flavour, the vegetables having given their all to the broth, emerging washed out, so soft and limp. The result of this disappointment is that a secondary set of carrots and leeks are separately cooked now, so retaining a touch of freshness and a better texture.

One final option: a split pig's trotter added to the initial, long cooking of the ham hocks. This makes for a richer broth, while also adding gelatine to the liquid. If you were not to make the soup, then any leftover ham could be chopped up, mixed with some of the (reduced) broth, chopped parsley added and then packed into pots. Once cold and jellied, this can be sliced and eaten with hot buttered toast and gherkins. And very nice it is, too.

Put the ham hocks into a roomy pot. Cover with cold water, bring up to the boil and then discard the water. Refill the pot with fresh water, to generously cover the hocks, and add the vegetables, bay leaves and peppercorns. Pour in the cider, bring to the boil, remove any scum that forms on the surface and simmer quietly for 1½ hours. Carefully lift out the hocks, put into a clean pot and strain the cooking liquor over them. Discard the vegetable debris. Keep the hocks warm, in their broth.

To cook the split peas, drain them and put in a large pan. Generously cover with some of the ham broth to a depth of about 2 finger joints. Don't add any salt, bring up to a simmer, remove any scum with kitchen paper, and cook until tender – about 35–40 minutes (you may need to add a touch more broth, or water, if the peas are not cooked before the broth has been absorbed). Meanwhile, put the carrots and leeks into another pan and also pour some of the ham broth over them, only just to cover, together with the butter. Put on a lid and cook until tender; about 20 minutes. Reheat the ham hocks in their remaining broth, then remove skin and fat if you wish (I like to keep some of these intact) and pull the meat off the bone.

To finish and serve the assembly, take 4 healthy servings of the split peas (keep some back for soup; see page 272), mix with the buttery carrots and leeks, season well and stir in the parsley. Take a large, heated deep serving dish, pile the peas and vegetables in the centre and arrange the pieces of ham hock around them, adding a little extra broth to moisten the dish, if necessary. A generous pot of freshly mixed English mustard is essential on the table too, for me.

pea & ham soup

....

serves 2

50g butter

1 small onion, chopped

400–500ml ham broth

3–4 tbsp cooked split peas
  (see previous recipe)

freshly ground white pepper

2–3 tbsp cream

a little shredded ham hock

1 tbsp chopped parsley

....

Melt the butter in a pan and stew the onion until soft and lightly coloured. Pour in the broth and add the peas. Bring up to a simmer and add the pepper; add salt only if necessary. Liquidise the soup, or, for a nicer, mealier texture, put it through a vegetable mill (mouli-légumes). Return to a clean pan, stir in the cream and gently reheat with the cooked ham and parsley.

crab & sweetcorn soup

....

serves 4

approx. 1kg cooked crab (a hen crab, if
   possible), in its shell

250ml Shaohsing Chinese rice wine

20g dried shiitake mushrooms

1 tbsp sesame oil – plus a little extra

100g fatty, streaky unsmoked bacon,
   chopped

2 cloves of garlic, chopped

1.5 litres chicken stock

2 star anise

2 fresh corn on the cob

1 large knob of fresh ginger, peeled and
   cut into thin slivers

2 spring onions, trimmed and very
   thinly sliced

a little chopped coriander leaf (optional)

....

I had always wanted to have a go at making a Chinese-style sweetcorn soup, but with freshly hulled corn from the cob and freshly picked crab meat, using the shells to make a stock in a European manner and then thickening the soup with the creamy roe (brown) meat. Well, it took some time to get it just right ... and here it is, just for you.

I further wanted to get right away from a cornflour-thickened soup that is the usual way with traditional Chinese soups such as these. I am not averse to this way of things; a wonderful hot and sour soup, for example, I would not wish for in any other way than that of viscous wobble, dark brown and steaming, with attendant vegetables and bean curd all caught up in bowl of sweat-inducing, vinegar-hot devil's brew. No, it was more of a pale broth that I was looking for. A lighter soup, maybe. Delicate? Yes, delicate is about right.

If you are familiar with preparing a freshly cooked crab, then proceed to so do. If not, ask a fishmonger to open up the central shell, so revealing the interior roe meat, and also ask him to crack the large claws; equally important, don't let him chuck away the shells! From then on, it is a relatively easy task to extract both the white and brown crab meat from its shell. Put both meats into separate dishes and keep cool in the fridge.

First things first, messy-wise: attempt to crack/chop the empty crab shells/bits into smallish pieces and put to one side.

Warm the rice wine in a small pan and put in the mushrooms. Allow to soak for at least 20 minutes, or until soft. Lift them out, thinly slice and put to one side, reserving the wine. Now, warm the sesame oil in a large pot and add the bacon and garlic. Quietly fry until pale golden, then tip in the crushed/chopped crab shells. Stir around for a bit, then allow to colour and infuse their flavour into the bacon fat, for about 10 minutes. Pour in the mushroom-infused rice wine and the chicken stock and pop in the star anise. Bring up to a simmer and cook together for about 1 hour; along the way, occasionally remove any fat that settles on the surface with several sheets of kitchen paper. Strain the mixture through a colander suspended over a clean pan, and leave to drain for at least 10 minutes. Discard all debris from the colander.

Remove the kernels from the corn cobs with a sharp knife, just cover with water (unsalted) and cook until tender – about 10 minutes. Leave in the cooking water and put to one side.

Now, place the brown meat in a small pan and add a ladle or two of the broth. Using a wand blender (or a small liquidiser), process the mixture until smooth and return to the broth. Stir together and then strain the entire mixture through a sieve; this makes sure that no trace of shell is apparent. Add the cooked corn (including its cooking water) and reserved sliced mushrooms to the broth, together with the ginger and spring onions. Bring up to a simmer, stir in the white crab meat just to heat through, then ladle into hot soup plates and sprinkle over the coriander, if using. Finally, shake a little extra sesame oil over the surface, as droplets.

lentil salad with soft-boiled egg & anchovy croûtes

....

serves 4

4 eggs (not too fresh, as very fresh ones
    are often more difficult to peel)

12 thin croutons cut from a baguette,
    lightly brushed with olive oil and
    baked until crisp

salt and freshly ground black pepper

1 tbsp finely chopped parsley

for the lentils

2 tbsp olive oil

4 rashers of smoked streaky bacon,
    finely diced

200g Puy lentils, washed

400ml water

½ a chicken stock cube

1 small onion, peeled and stuck
    with 3 cloves

1 bay leaf

for the anchovy paste

1 x 50g tin of anchovy fillets, drained
    of oil, finely chopped to mush

75g softened butter

1 tbsp olive oil

juice of ½ a lemon

a few shakes of Tabasco sauce

for the dressing

1 dsp Dijon mustard

1 dsp red wine vinegar

salt and freshly ground black pepper

1 small clove of garlic, crushed and
    finely chopped

75ml extra virgin olive oil

75ml peanut or other neutral oil

....

I think that I first assembled this pleasing, interestingly textured dish about seventeen years ago – and had completely forgotten about it, until now. I have always enjoyed lentils, particularly dressed as a warm salad. Anchovies – and as a paste with gusto, spread upon their crunchy croûtes – marry so well with these little pulses and, of course, are famously at home with eggs, too.

    And these eggs really should be soft-boiled, so that their runny yolks further help to dress the salad (think salade niçoise, and what runny egg yolk does to that delicious assembly). I know that eggs cooked like this can be tricky, but the method for cooking them here is, I think, pretty well foolproof.

To cook the lentils, heat the olive oil in a stainless steel pan and fry the bacon until crisp and golden. Add the lentils and stir well so that they are coated with fat. Pour in the water and add the ½ stock cube. Add the cloved onion and bay leaf, then gently simmer the lentils, uncovered, for 30–35 minutes, or so, until they are just cooked; be careful that they don't turn mushy, which they can suddenly do, so keep having occasional tastes. Remove the onion and bay leaf and allow the lentils to cool completely. Only now season with salt to taste.

To make the anchovy paste, mash together all the ingredients until smooth; use a small blender, if you wish. Put into the fridge to firm up.

To make the dressing, whisk the mustard, vinegar, salt, pepper and garlic together until well blended. Add the oils in a thin stream while still whisking, to homogenise the dressing; I sometimes add a little warm water to correct the consistency.

Put the eggs into a small pan and cover with cold water. Bring up to a full boil, switch off the heat, cover and leave for exactly 4 minutes. Rinse the eggs under cold water for a few minutes, drain and then carefully peel them; tricky, sometimes, when soft-boiled, and you may wish to go for an extra half minute, if nervous.

Warm the lentils through (drain off any excess cooking liquid if too wet), stir in the dressing, check seasoning and spoon on to 4 warmed plates. Spread the anchovy paste on to the croûtes and put 3 on each plate. Place an egg in the centre of the lentils, then take a sharp knife and cut it lengthways, so that the runny yolk pours out. Trickle over each serving a little extra olive oil, add a good grinding of pepper and sprinkle with the chopped parsley.

desserts & puddings

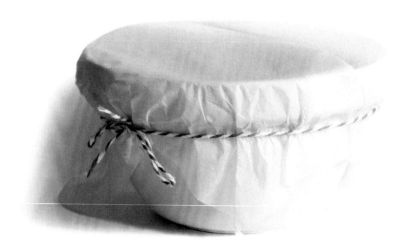

four puddings
& a crumble

a rich figgy pudding

serves 6

175g dried figs, chopped

100g sultanas

100g ginger preserve (or ginger marmalade),
  warmed until melted

1 tbsp sweet sherry or Madeira

1 tbsp Cognac

grated zest and juice of 1 small lemon

grated zest and juice of 1 small orange

100g self-raising flour

½ rounded tsp baking powder

good pinch of salt

75g fresh white breadcrumbs

75g suet

50g ground almonds

1 rounded tsp mixed spice

2 small eggs

2–3 tbsp milk

softened butter, for greasing

3 tbsp golden syrup

for the rum sauce

50g butter

40g plain flour

350ml cold milk

tiny pinch of salt

50–75g golden caster sugar, to taste

2–3 tbsp dark rum

50ml whipping cream

It is not often one finds dried figs in a pudding, but they have a really
rich flavour and a delicious, almost crunchy texture from the seeds within.
Naturally, this always reminds me of the old-fashioned fig rolls we were
given as children; not the most exciting of biscuits compared with other
more chocolatey biscuits, but they may have made us 'regular', at least …

Put the figs and sultanas into a bowl with the warmed ginger preserve, sherry or
Madeira, Cognac, and the zest and juice of the lemon and orange. Leave for 1 hour
to allow the fruits to soak up the alcohols.

Put the flour, baking powder, salt, breadcrumbs, suet, almonds and spice into, preferably, the bowl of an electric mixer. Beat the eggs together in a small bowl and stir into the soaked fruit. Switch on the machine at its lowest speed, then slowly pour in the egg/soaked fruit mixture until well mixed. Turn up the speed just a little, add some of the milk, and beat together for a minute or two, until a 'dropping' consistency is achieved when you lift out the beater.

Generously butter a 1-litre capacity pudding basin, pour in the syrup and, using a palette knife or spatula, spread the syrup right up the sides of the basin to coat it completely. Quickly pour the mixture into the basin and smooth the surface. Make a pleat across the centre of a lightly buttered sheet of kitchen foil (to allow for expansion), then wrap it around the top of the basin and tie with string. Place the pudding in a large saucepan (or steamer) and add enough water to come a third of the way up the basin. Put a lid on the pan, bring up to a simmer, and steam for 2 hours, checking now and then to ensure that the pan does not boil dry. Remove from the heat, turn the pudding out on to a warm serving dish and serve with the following rum sauce.

To make the sauce, take a small saucepan and in it melt the butter over a moderate heat. Stir in the flour until blended and quietly cook together for about a minute, keeping the mixture pale. Using a whisk, add the milk all in one go, mixing it in with vigour, until all is smooth. Continue whisking, more quietly now, until beginning to thicken, then switch to a wooden spoon, but continue stirring until fully thickened, for several more minutes. Add the salt, sugar and rum and, after a few more minutes, stir in the cream and bring to a final simmer. Keep warm, covered, until ready to serve with the pudding.

apple & mincemeat suet pudding

serves a greedy 4, or a more
  parsimonious 6

softened butter, for greasing

approx. 2 tbsp demerara sugar

a little semi-skimmed milk

clotted cream

for the suet pastry

250g self-raising flour

180g suet

¼ tsp salt

60g fresh white breadcrumbs

½ tsp baking powder

125–150ml semi-skimmed milk

for the filling

4 sweet apples (approx. 500g), Cox's,
  say, peeled and grated

grated zest and juice of 1 small lemon

200g mincemeat

pinch of ground cloves

big pinch of cinnamon

½ tsp ground ginger

1 tbsp Calvados (or Cognac)

Over the past few years, I have been taking the trouble to obtain fresh suet from an enterprising good butcher. Whenever he buys kidneys (either from veal or beef, but not lamb; too strong for puddings), I ask for the suet, bring it home and put it through a mincer. I then freeze it in plastic bags in 180g amounts. It is then ready to use, direct from frozen.

    The suet from around the kidney is the finest, in my view. Also, it produces the lightest suet pastry I know, together with a special flavour and richness. Do a little research and I feel sure you will be able find some from an accommodating butcher, somewhere. Otherwise, it will be have to be from those little red and yellow boxes, which are fine; just not quite the same.

Mix together the first 5 pastry ingredients in a large bowl (or in the bowl of an electric mixer, with the flat beater) using your hands. Add at least 125ml of the milk to achieve a cohesive mass, adding a little more if it is too sticky. Knead for a few minutes until it feels supple. Flatten to a fat disc and allow to relax for 30 minutes in the fridge. Meanwhile, to make the filling, simply mix all the ingredients together in a bowl and put to one side.

Roll out the pastry thickly, about 0.75cm, ending up with a large circle. Cut a wedge out of this circle (about a quarter) and put it to one side.

Now, thickly grease a 1-litre pudding basin with plenty of softened butter, then sprinkle over the demerara sugar and, moving the bowl around with your hands, allow the sugar to stick to the butter all over. Shake out any excess. Fit the pastry into the basin neatly and join it up, if possible, without too many wrinkles. Roll out the cut-out wedge, along with any trimmings from the large circle (once you have fitted it into the basin) to form a smaller circle for the lid.

Fill the pastry-lined bowl with the apple/mincemeat mixture, brush the edges of the pastry with milk, fix on the pastry lid and make a couple of holes in the top with a small knife, for steam to escape. As in the previous recipe, make a pleat across the centre of a lightly buttered sheet of kitchen foil (to allow for expansion), then wrap it around the top of the basin and tie with string. Place the pudding in a large saucepan (or steamer) and add enough water to come a third of the way up the basin. Put a lid on the pan and bring up to a simmer. This time, steam the pudding for 3 hours (suet pastry needs a longer cooking time), checking now and then to ensure that the pan does not boil dry.

Once cooked, turn the pudding out on to a hot serving dish and hand a lovely big bowl of clotted cream to melt over each serving.

sticky toffee pudding

serves 6

for the pudding

275ml boiling water

175g ready-chopped dates

1 rounded tsp bicarbonate of soda

50g salted butter

good pinch of salt

75g demerara sugar

75g molasses sugar

2 eggs

175g self-raising flour

1 tsp pure vanilla extract

softened butter, for greasing

for the sticky toffee topping

250ml double cream

80g salted butter

80g molasses sugar

for the extra sauce

300ml whipping cream

50g molasses sugar

50g salted butter

to serve

ice-cold double cream (optional)

I recall first noticing the recipe for STP in a cookery book compiled in 1971 by *The Good Food Guide*, full of excellent dishes supplied by those fortunate enough to have been included in the *Guide* of the previous year. The recipe belonged to a Mrs Martin of the Old Rectory in Claughton, Lancashire. Having then ignored it for years, it was not until some time in the mid 1980s, while visiting Sharrow Bay Hotel on Lake Ullswater, in the English Lakes, that I noticed STP on their luncheon menu (it was always 'luncheon', at Sharrow). This was the first time I had ever seen the recipe cooked in a restaurant anywhere, but it turned out that STP had been a Sharrow fixture since around about the early to mid 1970s. And, as there is no mention of it in *Good Food Guides* previous to 1976, and as it is referred to as 'justly famous', I can only assume the legendary chef and co-proprietor, Francis Coulson, must have once read Mrs Martin's recipe, too.

He certainly improved on the original, making the truly scrumptious Sharrow version his very own, very British pudding. But, alas, here is the ironic crunch: the original STP recipe comes from North America – and Canada, to be precise. And I know this because when I had once given a recipe for STP (the one here has changed since then) in a newspaper column, some years ago now,

the late Mrs Martin's son made contact, informing me that the recipe had originally been given to his mother by a Canadian friend. Well, geddaway.

Over the years, so obsessed have I become with the STP that I can bore for England over it. For those who know the recipe well, it is clearly a batter, not a cake mix. This, of course, should have given the game away re. its origins ages ago: the raising agents alone smack of US muffin mixes. Naturally, this is why the pudding rises so helpfully, every single time. Nevertheless, the most important ingredient of all is the dates.

Anyone who thinks that these can be substituted with, say, dried apricots, figs, prunes, bananas (for Heaven's sake!), etc. are bewildered folk. Dates are sticky and sweet, adding their enormously rich texture to an otherwise basic mix. And those who add nuts are, well ... nuts. Why on earth would one want an interruptive crunch in something so soft and luscious? (I have the same low opinion of those who also think nuts now seem to be a good idea in a Christmas pudding.) Finally, never serve an STP with ice cream; it is far too sweet.

Preheat the oven to 180°C/350°F/gas mark 4.

Measure the water from a boiled kettle, pour into a bowl and add the dates. Stir and leave until lukewarm. Meanwhile, measure out all the other pudding ingredients, add to the dates and water and stir together. Put this into the bowl of a food processor or liquidiser and purée until nearly smooth, but with a few tell-tale specks of date still visible. Generously butter a baking dish of at least 2-litre capacity on all surfaces and pour in the sponge batter. (Note: it is important that the chosen dish will be filled no more than half-full by the mixture, as it rises a great deal during cooking and you will need room to pour over the topping.) Bake for about 30 minutes, or until just firm to the touch.

Meanwhile, make both the topping and the extra sauce, by heating the ingredients gently in individual pans, whisking regularly, until they briefly boil and then smoothly amalgamate; two pans of butterscotch sauce, effectively. Pour the topping over the cooked pudding and place under a moderate grill until bubbling and sticky-looking. Spoon into individual bowls and pour around the extra sauce. The cold double cream, even though you might think it otiose, offers a very nice, cooling contrast to all that hot, sticky sponge and sweet, saucy sauces.

rice pudding

....

serves 4

40g butter

75g caster sugar

100g pudding rice (or Spanish paella rice)

½ a vanilla pod, split lengthways

1 litre full-cream milk

150ml double cream

pinch of salt

plenty of freshly grated nutmeg

....

For this cook, a proper, carefully made rice pudding is the glory of all British milk puddings. It is an intensely lactic arrangement of two perfect partners, so simply wedded that it almost beggars belief. I don't understand the inclusion of egg yolks to thicken it; nor do I like it made in the style of a risotto, though quite popular, these days. No, that which truly appeals to me is the quietly slow absorption of what seems to be a tiny amount of rice, by a veritable flood of milk, left to get on all by itself until sporting a delicate, golden-brown skin and all wobbly beneath. And, together with that enticing fragrance of nutmeg and vanilla … Well, it is, quite simply, a gorgeous thing.

Preheat the oven to 150°C/300°F/ gas mark 2.

Melt the butter in a solid-based, flameproof casserole and add the sugar. Stir around and heat gently until gooey, then add the rice and vanilla pod, and continue stirring until the rice looks a touch puffed and sticky with sugar. Now, gently pour in the milk, which will seethe around the rice causing the volatile rice/butter/sugar mixture to set into lumps at once. However, fear not, for as you stir around in this milky mess with the aid of a wooden spoon, within minutes any sugary lumps will soon dissolve into the milk as it heats up. Continuing to stir, add the cream and salt, and bring the mixture to a simmer. Once this is reached, give the mixture a final stir and grate at least a third of a nutmeg over the surface (do not stir again). Pop into the oven and bake for about 60–90 minutes; if the surface burnishes too quickly, lay a loose sheet of kitchen foil over the pudding. Once there is a very nice, thin, tarpaulin-like skin on the surface and the pudding only just wobbles in the centre, it is ready; remember, the rice will continue cooking a little as the heat wanes within. Serve at room temperature.

rhubarb crumble with Guernsey cream

···

serves 4

700g rhubarb

2 tbsp golden caster sugar

juice of ½ a lemon

several thin flakes of unsalted butter

a little extra golden caster sugar,
   for sprinkling

for the crumble mixture

250g very cold unsalted butter,
   cut into small chunks

400g plain flour

200g golden caster sugar

generous pinch of salt

to serve

Guernsey (or Jersey) cream

···

Let's be honest about this: a crumble mix is nothing more than unmixed pastry, and all the better for that. I don't believe in anything else, here, other than this traditional mix of butter, sugar and plain flour. No nuts. No oats. No 'bits', in other words. A pinch of salt is an imperative and should not be omitted. Finally, never make the mistake of patting/pressing the crumble mixture down, once piled on to the fruit. I like to carefully apply it in large spoonfuls, so allowing the mixture to trickle around the fruit, while also forming tiny hillocks so that, once cooked, the sugary-buttery-fruit juices nicely bubble up and around all over the place, especially at the edge of the dish, where they occasionally burn a bit. Very nice indeed, that.

Preheat the oven to 180°C/350°F/gas mark 4.

Place all the ingredients for the crumble mixture in a roomy bowl. Deftly, using your fingertips, rub the butter into the flour, sugar and salt, while lifting and dropping the mixture back through the fingers, so handling the ingredients as little as possible – in the same way as one begins to make pastry.

Pile the rhubarb into a buttered dish, sprinkle with sugar, squeeze over the lemon juice and distribute the flakes of butter over the fruit. Cover the fruit with the crumble mixture, sprinkle over a little extra golden caster sugar and place in the oven. Bake for about 40 minutes, or until jammy juices are oozing up around the edges of the dish, and the surface is pock-marked with golden pustules. Serve with lovely and thick Guernsey, or Jersey cream – and unpasteurised, if you can find it.

two sponges

with a turnover

apricot & almond turnovers

serves 4

20 dried apricots, approx. 150g

375g puff pastry, preferably in a sheet

75g marzipan

20 whole, skinned almonds

1 tbsp ground almonds

a few shakes of ground ginger

1 tbsp golden caster sugar

25–35g softened butter

1 small egg, beaten

caster sugar, to glaze

These flaky little pastries are an original idea, for me – and there are not many times when this happens. I guess that they may have once been inspired by a particularly good apricot Danish, but I remain unsure. However, they are devilishly good to eat.

Pour 350ml of boiling water over the apricots and leave to soak for at least 1 hour. Drain well, discarding the water. Divide the puff pastry into 4 pieces and roll out thinly (approx. 17–18cm square). Leave them to relax for 10 minutes in the fridge. Then, using a saucer, cut out 4 circles, not less than about 16cm in diameter.

Preheat the oven to 190°C/375°F/gas mark 5. Meanwhile, take an apricot, open it up with a small knife to form a pocket, push in a small nugget of marzipan, together with an almond, then push the apricot together again. Repeat with the remaining apricots and place them on a large plate lined with a double fold of kitchen paper.

In a small bowl, mix together the ground almonds, ground ginger and sugar. Sprinkle a quarter this mixture over one half of each pastry circle, and arrange 5 stuffed apricots over this. Dot the apricots with small smears of the butter. Now, brush the edge of each circle with a little of the beaten egg and fold over the pastry to make a semicircle. Using a fork, crimp the edges together. Now brush the top surface with the remaining egg, sprinkle generously with caster sugar and make 2 small holes in the top with the point of a knife for steam to escape. Place on a greased baking sheet and cook on the middle shelf of the oven for 25–30 minutes, or until crisp, puffed and golden. Allow to cool on a wire rack for about 5 minutes before eating. Serve with whipped cream (see page 309).

steamed ginger sponge

....

serves a generous 4

100g self-raising flour

2 rounded tsp ground ginger

1 tsp mixed spice

1 rounded tsp bicarbonate of soda

100g suet

100g fresh breadcrumbs

165g jar preserved stem ginger

scant 200ml milk

50g golden syrup

75g treacle (or molasses)

pinch of salt

1 large egg, beaten

softened butter, for greasing

....

This wickedly lovely pudding makes regular lunchtime appearances at our restaurant, Bibendum. I have always been fond of ginger puddings of any kind, but was happily astonished on one particular occasion when the very famous French chef Alain Ducasse (he with an absurd amount of Michelin rosettes to his name) came to dine. He so enjoyed this most British kind of pudding that he asked for the recipe. So I furnished him with it, and a great pleasure it was to so do.

Note: you may wish to make individual puddings here, using dariole molds. If so, reduce the cooking time by 30 minutes.

Sift the flour into a mixing bowl with the spices and bicarbonate of soda. Add the suet and breadcrumbs and mix well. Coarsely chop the stem ginger, including its syrup, in the bowl of a food processor. Warm the milk with half the mass of chopped stem ginger, the golden syrup, the treacle or molasses and a pinch of salt. Beat into the dry ingredients, with the egg, until sloppy and just dropping off the spoon.

Generously grease a 1-litre pudding basin with butter and put the remaining half of the chopped ginger mass in the bottom. Pour in the pudding mixture, cover with buttered and pleated kitchen foil, tie round with string and steam for 2 hours. Turn out on to a dish and serve with very cold thick cream or custard (see Marmalade Sponge with Cointreau Custard, page 296, omitting the orange liqueur).

marmalade sponge with Cointreau custard

....

serves 4

for the sponge

175g thin-cut marmalade, warmed

100g butter, at room temperature

100g caster sugar

2 large eggs, beaten

grated zest and juice of 2 large lemons

150g self-raising flour

pinch of salt

1 level tsp baking powder

for the orange custard

300ml milk

½ a vanilla pod, split lengthways

4 egg yolks

40g caster sugar

2 tbsp Cointreau or Grand Marnier

....

Mum used to make many such sponges as this one when I was little. Jam, mostly, was the favourite sticky bit, but previously stewed apples, plums and gooseberries – not all at once – made seasonal appearances. The custard was always from Mr Bird, but we loved it all the same; doesn't everyone, if truth be told? However, it really is worth making the real McCoy, here, especially with the addition of an orange liqueur. A grown-up custard, to be sure.

You will need a round or oval baking dish, about 5cm deep, with a capacity of around 1 litre, well buttered and the base lined with a fitted sheet of dampened greaseproof paper.

Preheat the oven to 180°C/350°F/gas mark 4.

Pour the marmalade over the greaseproof paper in the baking dish and allow it to settle and cool. Cream the butter and sugar together until light and fluffy. Add the eggs, a little at a time, beating until really thick and white. Add the lemon zest and sift in the flour, salt and baking powder. Fold in carefully, along with the lemon juice. It should be of a dropping consistency.

Pile the sponge mixture over the marmalade, level off with a spatula and bake
for 30–35 minutes, or until well puffed up, golden and firm. Check with a skewer –
it should emerge clean. Allow to cool in the dish for 10 minutes.

To make the orange custard, heat the milk together with the vanilla pod in a heavy-
bottomed saucepan. Remove from the stove and whisk for a few seconds to release
the vanilla seeds into the milk. Briefly beat together the egg yolks and sugar. Strain
the hot milk into the beaten egg and sugar, whisking as you go. Return to the
saucepan and cook over a very low heat until limpid and lightly thickened. Add the
chosen liqueur, give the custard a final vigorous whisk to fully amalgamate and
then pour into a warm jug. (Note: if you are unlucky enough to split the custard,
a quick blast in a liquidiser will rescue the drama.)

To serve the sponge, run a knife carefully around the edge, turn it out on to
a serving dish and remove the greaseproof paper. Offer the custard at table.

chocolate, coffee & custard & a small meringue

coffee ice cream

....

serves 4

75g espresso coffee beans

400ml full-cream milk

150ml double cream

50g powdered milk

50g liquid glucose

85g golden caster sugar

pinch of salt

a dribble of vanilla extract

....

In my opinion, ice creams are not ice creams unless manually or electrically processed until churned to that correct, very smooth 'cream'. The suggestion of occasionally whisking about a bit, breaking down the ice crystals every half an hour or so, is as far away from the nomenclature 'ice cream' as it is possible to think. If you like homemade ice cream as much as do I, then having a good machine in the kitchen – albeit an expensive outlay – will, I promise you, be a worthwhile investment.

The following recipe may, initially, appear to be completely bonkers, especially if you regularly make ice cream using a custard base, i.e. egg yolks, milk, cream, sugar and vanilla. That which you are about to read, however, is, as far as I am led to believe, the basis for almost all Italian gelati. What is truly astonishing, of course, is the very ease of making this ice cream. Although this particular one is flavoured with coffee, it could be as basic a vanilla ice cream as you would want it to be; just omit the coffee and its infusion, and up the vanilla. Liquid glucose is to be found in the baking section of almost all supermarkets.

Note: do not be tempted to grind the coffee beans for this particular recipe, for it is the pale colour and delicate flavour from whole beans which give it its charm.

Put the coffee beans into a pan and pour over the milk and cream. Bring up to a simmer, then stir in the other ingredients using a stout whisk and vigorously, if you like – to promote flavour from the coffee beans, further bruising them towards the liquid, for maximum flavour. Remove from the heat and leave to cool. Pour into a plastic, securely lidded box, place in the fridge and leave to infuse overnight. I like to shake the container as a maraca, occasionally, to entice the finest coffee flavour into the mixture.

The next day, strain the liquid from the beans and churn, in an ice cream machine, according to the manufacturer's instructions.

orange caramel custard

....

serves 4

120g granulated sugar

finely grated zest of 4 large, very
   orange oranges

500ml full-cream milk
   (Channel Islands, if possible)

75g caster sugar

3 whole eggs

4 egg yolks

....

I once had a very interesting conversation over dinner with a fellow chef (we had only just met, but I instantly liked him enormously), who had just cooked dinner for me and some colleagues. To be truthful, the conversation ended up being quite a vociferous exchange of opinions. To some it may have sounded petty, the point I was trying to make, but it concerned restraint where this little wobble of a dessert was concerned.

Chris had chosen to accompany his truly perfect crème caramel (caramel custard) with a 'tuile', a thin, French-style biscuit sometimes also called, as a smaller version, a 'langue de chat' (cat's tongue). Now then, when this custard emerged as flawless as did his offering, I could see absolutely no point in adding anything else to it at all. I think I may have said, 'It simply gets in the way, even if you chose not to eat it!' And he may have countered, quite rightly, 'Well don't, then!' I then replied, 'Ah, but you see, someone who may never have eaten something so good, so impeccably made, so smooth and creamy as yours, might be fooled into thinking that a crunch on a biscuit will improve it.' It won't. Believe me. Just leave it alone. And *please* eat with a teaspoon.

Note: you will need 4 large dariole moulds (or ramekins) of approx. 175ml.

Put the granulated sugar into a solid-based saucepan and add 3–4 tablespoons of water. Bring to a simmer and cook slowly until the sugar has turned to a richly coloured caramel; take care during the final stages, so as not to burn it. Pour into the base of the dariole moulds (or ramekins), dividing the caramel between them. Leave to cool.

Preheat the oven to 150°C/300°F/gas mark 2.

Put the orange zest, milk and caster sugar into a stainless steel saucepan and warm together, occasionally stirring, until just below simmering point. Switch off the heat, cover with a lid and leave to infuse for at least 1 hour. Put the eggs and yolks into a roomy bowl, beat together lightly and then strain over the orange-infused milk. Gently beat together, but not vigorously; the last thing you want is for too much froth to form on the surface. Ladle the mixture into the caramel-lined moulds and fill to the brim. Place them in a deep roasting tin and fill with tap-hot water, so that it rises about three-quarters of the way up the outside of the moulds. Carefully slide the tin into the oven and loosely lay a sheet of kitchen foil flat over the surface of the moulds, but don't secure it down. Bake in the oven for about 40–45 minutes, until the custards are just set – lightly press a finger on the surface, or give them a little shake; they should gently wobble.

Remove from the oven, take out of the roasting tin and leave to cool. When quite cold, cover each mould with a small sheet of clingfilm and put into the fridge for at least 2 hours. To unmould, run a small knife around the edge of each custard and up-end on to individual, shallow dishes. The caramel will surround the custards, with the top of each one sporting a pretty, golden tan. Eat with teaspoons, nice and slowly.

ginger chocolate pot

....

serves 6

150ml double cream

½ a vanilla pod, split in half lengthways

125g dark chocolate (70% cocoa),
  broken into pieces

100ml milk

2 egg yolks

1 heaped tbsp icing sugar

1 rounded tsp ground ginger

4–5 globes of preserved stem ginger,
  chopped into small pieces

several tsp ginger syrup (from the jar)

....

This little pot of rich chocolate is an old favourite of mine – and, blessedly, also enjoyed by many others. This time, however, its outing here has been embellished by a touch of ginger. The inspiration was to quietly catch a similar moment of biting into ginger chocolate.

Preheat the oven to 140°C/275°F/gas mark 1.

Warm the cream with the vanilla pod, whisk for a moment to disperse the seeds, then cover and leave to infuse for 30 minutes. Meanwhile, in a small saucepan, quietly melt the chocolate in the milk. Beat the egg yolks, icing sugar and ground ginger together until fluffy, then incorporate the chocolate/milk mixture and vanilla-infused cream and blend together thoroughly. Pass through a fine sieve into a jug.

Place the chopped ginger and a little ginger syrup in the bottom of 6 ramekins or small porcelain pots, then pour in the chocolate mixture from the jug until each pot is almost full. Put them into a deep roasting tin and pour in enough tap-hot water to come at least two-thirds up the side of the pots. Bake for 45–60 minutes, or until slightly puffed up and spongy to the touch of a finger. Remove from the oven, allow to cool for a few moments, then lift the pots from the water on to a clean tray. Refrigerate for at least 6 hours before serving. If you wish, eat with a little ice-cold pouring cream spooned into each pot.

coffee granita

···

serves 4
120g caster sugar
600ml strong, hot espresso coffee

···

With a recipe that involves only two ingredients, there might not seem much to say when attempting to explain the beauty of this icy-cold crystal mass of frozen coffee; well, there, I've said it. Ironically, of course, that which I explained with reference to the making of a smooth Italian gelato (see Coffee Ice Cream on page 299) is exactly what is not wanted, here. A fork is always the best utensil for forming granita crystals, so don't be tempted to use a whisk, which will make too fine a texture. Also, regular visits to the freezer to quietly coax the crystals from the liquid are important steps (cook a nicely involved stew, or something similar, at the same time, so keeping kitchen attendance levels high); allowing the liquid to freeze to a block, then scraping away at it, will result in a fine powder, not the exquisite crystals which are the delight of a great granita.

Put a shallow metal tray (about 1 litre capacity) into the freezer before you do anything else.

Stir the sugar into the coffee. Allow to become completely cold. Pour into the chilled tray and place in the freezer. Leave in there for about 40 minutes. Have a look and if there are any ice crystals forming around the edge, gently bring them into the liquid centre using a fork; if not, leave for a little longer before returning to the scene. Have another look again in about 20 minutes and repeat this forking about business. Keep doing this until the entire mixture is a mass of coffee crystals with no remaining liquid parts. Once this has been achieved, tip the granita into a plastic, lidded box and store in the freezer until needed. Serve in pre-chilled glasses with whipped cream (see Small Meringues with Whipped Cream, page 309).

small meringues with whipped cream

....

serves 4–6

for the meringues

4 egg whites

pinch of salt

225g caster sugar

a little softened butter, for greasing

plain flour

for the whipped cream

300ml double cream, preferably Jersey
    or Guernsey

1 tbsp icing sugar

1 tsp vanilla extract

....

Ah, lovely, lovely meringues – and a return to Mum's Aga. She used to make them in the bottom oven, from where they emerged after about two hours as golden and sweet-smelling, together with very tiny explosions of caramel dotted about their crazed and almost mountainous surfaces; they were big, Mum's meringues.

Nowadays, I prefer mine a little more dainty and, like hers, they still turn out golden-ish, but maybe a touch paler; the solid fuel Aga's bottom oven temperature was a fluctuating affair and, together with an occasional moment of forgetfulness on her part, produced very golden meringues indeed, sometimes. Nevertheless, the unpasteurised cream (from the next-door-but-one farm), lightly sweetened, whipped to soft peaks and used to sandwich the meringues, would always save the day.

Preheat the oven to 140°C/275°F/gas mark 1.

Using a scrupulously clean mixing bowl, whip the egg whites with the salt until soft but able to hold a peak. Beat in the sugar, a tablespoon at a time, until glossy and stiff.

Lightly grease a flat baking tray with the butter and sift over a spoonful of flour. Shake around a bit to disperse the flour in an even coating and then tap off the

excess (the kitchen sink is the most contained area and affords the least mess). I have always found this coating to be the most effective non-stick method, however arcane you might think it. And I loathe fiddling about with baking parchment.

Spoon out the meringue mixture on to the baking tray with whichever size spoon you like (a dessertspoon is my choice). Bake in the oven for about 1–1½ hours. I like my meringues with a pale golden hue. Leave to cool for a few minutes before removing them from the baking tray and placing them on a wire rack to cool.

Whip the cream with the sugar and vanilla until thick, then use this generously to sandwich the meringues together. Eat with a dainty fork.

Conversion chart

Weight

15g	½oz	250g	9oz	850g	1lb 14oz
20g	¾oz	275g	10oz	900g	2lb
25g	1oz	310g	11oz	950g	2lb 2oz
40g	1½oz	350g	12oz	1kg	2¼lb
50g	2oz	375g	13oz	1.4kg	3lb
65g	2½oz	400g	14oz	1.5kg	3lb 5oz
75g	3oz	450g	1lb	1.6kg	3½lb
90g	3½oz	500g	1lb 2oz	1.7kg	3¾lb
110g	4oz	550g	1¼lb	1.8kg	4lb
125g	4½oz	600g	1lb 5oz	2kg	4½lb
150g	5oz	650g	1lb 7oz	2.3kg	5lb
175g	6oz	700g	1½lb	2.5kg	5½lb
200g	7oz	750g	1lb 10oz	2.7kg	6lb
225g	8oz (½lb)	800g	1lb 12oz	3kg	6½lb

Volume

Metric	Imperial				
25ml	1fl oz	400ml	14fl oz	2 litres	3½ pints
50ml	2fl oz	450ml	¾ pint	2.1 litres	3¾ pints
75ml	3fl oz	500ml	18fl oz	2.3 litres	4 pints
90ml	3½fl oz	600ml	1 pint	2.75 litres	4¾ pints
100ml	4fl oz	750ml	1¼ pints	3.4 litres	6 pints
125ml	4½fl oz	900ml	1½ pints	3.9 litres	7 pints
150ml	5fl oz (¼ pint)	1 litre	1¾ pints	4.5 litres	8 pints (1 gallon)
175ml	6fl oz	1.1 litres	2 pints		
200ml	7fl oz	1.25 litres	2¼ pints		
225ml	8fl oz	1.4 litres	2½ pints		
250ml	9fl oz	1.6 litres	2¾ pints	teaspoon (tsp) = 5ml	
300ml	10fl oz (½ pint)	1.75 litres	3 pints	dessert spoon (dsp) = 10ml	
350ml	12fl oz	1.8 litres	3¼ pints	tablespoon (tbsp) = 15ml	

Oven temperatures

				190°C	Fan 170°C	375°F	Gas Mark 5
140°C	Fan 120°C	275°F	Gas Mark 1	200°C	Fan 180°C	400°F	Gas Mark 6
150°C	Fan 130°C	300°F	Gas Mark 2	220°C	Fan 200°C	425°F	Gas Mark 7
160°C	Fan 140°C	325°F	Gas Mark 3	230°C	Fan 210°C	450°F	Gas Mark 8
180°C	Fan 160°C	350°F	Gas Mark 4	240°C	Fan 220°C	475°F	Gas Mark 9

Index

A

aioli 194–7
almond & apricot turnovers 293
anchovy
    & onion tarts 15–17
    croûtes 276–7
    mayonnaise 237–9
    piedmontese pepper 84–5
    salade niçoise 21–3
    sauce 18–19
    tartare dressing 247–8
apple
    & mincemeat suet pudding 283–4
    sauce 190–3
apricot & almond turnovers 293
Asian green sauce 129–31
asparagus
    anchovy mayonnaise & veal fillet 237–9
    délices d'Argenteuil 165–7
aubergine
    & tomatoes with homemade masala paste 29–31
    parmigiana 27–8
    with olive oil, garlic, parsley & feta cheese 25–6
avocado, jalapeños & chopped prawns on toast 204–5

B

bacon
    crab & sweetcorn soup 273–5
    lentil salad 276–7
    pigeon & mushroom pie 184–7
    potato soup 261–2
    quiche Lorraine 170–1
baked
    pappardelle, pancetta & porcini 91–3
    trout, Chablis, cream & tarragon 72–3
beef
    Carpaccio 225–7
    tripe, spring onions, ginger, chillies & coriander 230–2
beetroot & horseradish relish for salt ox tongue 44–5
biscuits, Parmesan 60–1
braised neck of lamb with carrots & pearl barley 117–19
bread & tomato Tuscan salad 77–9
breadcrumbs 124–5
breast of lamb baked with onions 120–3
broad bean, salad of, smoked cod's roe, ricotta & olive oil 80–1
buttered rice, mozzarella, garlic & basil 138–9

C

calf's liver & sweet & sour onions 242–3
caramel orange custard 301–3
Carpaccio 225–7
carrot, pearl barley & lamb 117–19
cep, parsley, garlic & grilled veal chop 240–1
Chablis, cream, tarragon & baked trout 72–3
cheese
    & ham fried sandwich 168–9
    Lancashire, & onion pie, My Mother's 55–6
    sauce 47–8
    white wine, mustard & pork chops 67
    see also feta; mozzarella; Parmesan; ricotta; Roquefort
chicken
    coq au vin 68–70
    homemade tandoori 150–1
    hot salad, with sweet mustard dressing 148–9
    poached, with saffron sauce & cucumber 145–7
chicken liver
    & pork terrine & green peppercorns 157–9
    mousse & port jelly 154–6
    & mushrooms on toast 153
    pilau 160–1
chicory, Roquefort & pear salad with walnut oil 62–3
chive butter sauce 107–9
chocolate ginger pot 304–5
chopped prawns, avocado & jalapeños, on toast 204–5
cod's roe
    smoked, ricotta, olive oil & broad beans salad 80–1
    see also salt cod
coffee
    granita 306–7
    ice cream 299–300
Cointreau custard 296–7
coq au vin 68–70
    gravy, poached eggs in 71
cotechino sausage, lentils & mustard fruits 175–7
crab & sweetcorn soup 273–5
croquettes, spinach & ricotta 18–19
croûtes, anchovy 276–7
croutons 86–7
crumble, rhubarb, & Guernsey cream 290–1
cucumber
    fried, soured cream & dill 35–7
    gazpacho 86–7
    saffron sauce & poached chicken 145–7
    salad 101–2
    tzatziki 38–9
custard

Cointreau 296–7
orange caramel 301–3

D
date, sticky toffee pudding 285–7
délices d'Argenteuil 165–7
duck, English roast, & apple sauce 190–3

E
egg
poached, in coq au vin gravy 71
poached, with Lancashire cheese, leeks & chives 57
quiche Lorraine 170–1
Roquefort tart 64–5
salade niçoise 21–3
smoked haddock pilaf 105–6
soft-boiled, anchovy croûtes & lentil salad 276–7
endive
& pot-roast pork 49–51
au gratin 47–8

F
feta & aubergine 25–6
figgy pudding, rich 181–2
fillet of veal, anchovy mayonnaise & asparagus 237–9
fish
with a white butter sauce 213–15
see also specific fish
flageolet bean & warm prawn salad 206–7
fried
cucumber, soured cream & dill 35–7
ham & cheese sandwich 168–9
fruit
mustard 175–7
see also specific fruit

G
garlic
mayonnaise 124–5
mushrooms 96–7
gazpacho 86–7
ginger
chocolate pot 304–5
steamed sponge 294–5
gnocchi, potato, butter, sage, garlic & pine kernels 262–4
granita, coffee 306–7
grape & pot-roast quail 181–3
gravadlax, homemade, cucumber salad & mustard sauce 101–2
gravy

coq au vin 71
orange 198–9
greens, wilted, wrapped in Parma ham 82–3
gremolata 172–4
grilled
lamb cutlets & minted hollandaise 126–8
squab pigeon, sweet sherry vinegar & shallot vinaigrette 188–9
veal chop, ceps, parsley and garlic 240–1

H
haddock see smoked haddock
ham
& pea soup 272
endives au gratin 47–8
fried, & cheese sandwich 168–9
hock, & split peas 269–71
see also Parma ham
hollandaise sauce 107–9, 165–7
minted 126–8
homemade
gravadlax, cucumber salad & mustard sauce 101–2
tandoori chicken 150–1
horseradish
& beetroot relish for salt ox tongue 44–5
base recipe 41
cream 42–3
hot chicken salad with sweet mustard dressing 148–9

I
ice cream, coffee 299–300
Irish creamed shrimps on butter-grilled toast 203

J
jalapeño, avocado & chopped prawns on toast 204–5

K
kidney, potato & steak pie 228–9
kipper & tomato baked in cream 113

L
lamb
braised neck of, with carrots & pearl barley 117–19
breast, baked with onions 120–3
grilled cutlets, & minted hollandaise 126–8
leftover cold breast, sliced, breadcrumbed & fried till crisp, with garlic mayonnaise 124–5
marinated butterflied leg, & Asian green sauce

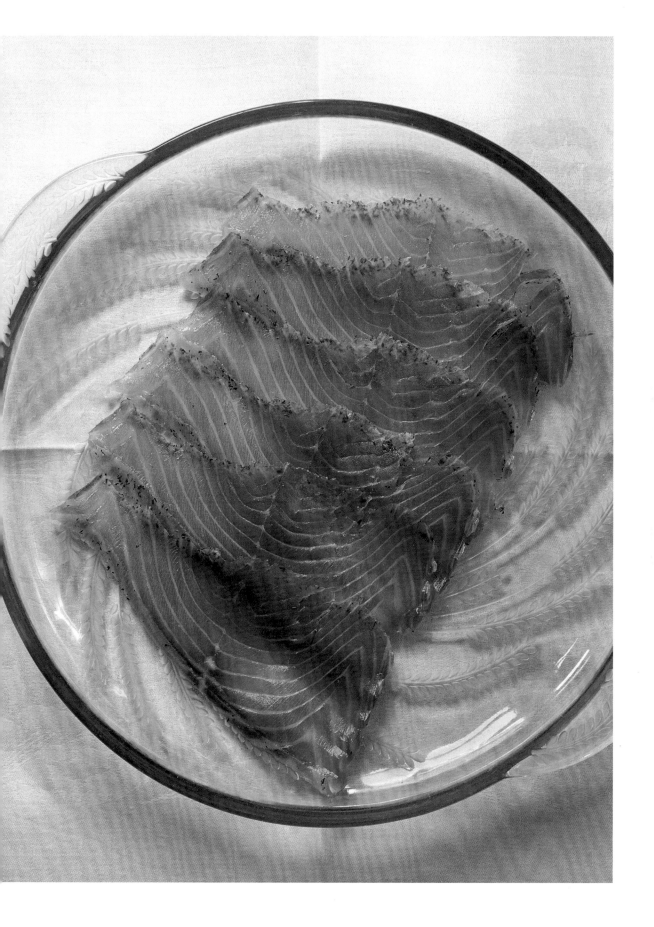

Acknowledgements

This book would not have been possible without the encouragement and help from those at BBC Books: Muna Reyal, Will Webb, Ed Griffiths, Annie Lee, Helen Everson and, of course, Fiona MacIntyre. It was a pleasure to be given the time and opportunity to write a cookery book with them.

Jason Lowe helped a bit too, I guess, taking lots of pictures in my home for some reason, while also generally getting in the way while I attempted to cook some nice food.

So much thanks, also, to those frankly bonkers folk at BBC Bristol who bravely took me on almost unseen. I would further like to praise their encouragement, help, patience and their downright good fun as genial folk to be around. Here they are …

Production: Pete Lawrence, Simon 'Swarthy' Knight, Simon Kerfoot, Michelle Crowley, Maria Norman, James Thompson, Richard Hanmer and Helen Shields.

Crew: Richard Hill, Conor Connolly, Billy Harron, Robbie Johnson, Sheree Jewell, Cheryl Martin, Gary Nagle and Peter Gordon. And Gavin.

Also, my admiration knows no bounds in consideration of Gary Skipton and Angela Maddick, who worked their magic in the editing suite.

At David Higham, I would like to say a big thank you to Georgina Ruffhead, who held my hand so warmly with my first television contract. Also, to Georgia Glover, who has always been a special, constant presence when any important matters arise.

And, finally, blessings to Jay Hunt and Ian Blandford who, each in differing ways, introduced me to the possibility of the small screen. I must introduce them to each other sometime...